Stippy

Susie

Great-grandpa

Uncle Edward

PETER AND HIS CAMERA

PETER AND HIS CAMERA

Told by Günter Spitzing and Dr. Karl Steinorth
Translated by Rolf Fricke

Illustrated by Hannelore Radetzky

Published by INPHO, Düsseldorf
1967

© Morgan & Morgan, Inc., 1973 (English translation)
Second Printing, 1974 (Published for Eastman Kodak Company)

All rights reserved in all countries.
No part of this book may be reproduced in
any form, including microfilming, or
translated without permission in writing
from the authors and publisher.

Reviewed by Kodak's Editors.
Distributed by Consumer Markets Division.

Rochester, New York 14650

Library of Congress Catalog
Card Number 72-83110
International Standard Book Number 0-87100-032-6

Printed in U.S.A.

Contents

Uncle Edward's Present	7
Great-Grandfather Tells a Story	15
Peter Takes His Uncle to the Train	32
Chasing an Astronaut with Reporter Kelly	39
At the Camera Store	55
Peter Helps the Police	60
Photography in Space	71
Class Trip to Mountainview Castle	78
What Peter Does to Take Good Pictures	90
Terms Used by Camera Fans	91

Uncle Edward's present

"Skippy, Skippy! Where are you hiding, you silly dog?" Peter stood in front of his house and shouted so loudly that his voice echoed all over Maple Street.

"Dear Skippy, good Skippy, please, please, come here!" begged his little sister Susie, and you could see by her face that she was about to cry. Skippy, the cutest, wooliest dog you could imagine had disappeared without a trace.

But wait—was that a whimper they heard? Yes, it was! The sound was coming from the basement! As fast as they could go, Peter and Susie ran down the stairs. And sure enough, there was Skippy. The little dog was sitting right on top of a huge pile of coal. How happy he was to see the children! He jumped around, sending a cloud of black coal dust into the air. Peter carried the wriggling little animal down from the coal pile, and Susie hugged the puppy in her arms. Upstairs in the house, everyone was waiting for them.

"You found the little runaway," said his father. At first, Mother was happy too, but all at once she put her hands to her face and exclaimed, "Heavens, what happened to you, Skippy, and to you, too, Susie?"

Their adventure in the basement had turned Skippy's fur a new color. He was now pitch black, and he looked just like the brush of a chimney sweep. Coal dust flew all over when he shook himself. And everyone could see by looking at her that Susie had held the dirty little puppy in her arms. Father laughed and said, "You both really look funny. Somebody should take a picture."

But Mother simply put Susie's clothes into the washing machine, little Susie in the bathtub, and Skippy in a pail of soapy water.

Fortunately, the excitement about Skippy had already ended when the doorbell rang. Peter opened it. "Uncle Edward, what a surprise! Mom, Dad, Susie! Uncle Edward is here!" The visitor received a warm welcome. Even Skippy seemed glad to see the guest, especially when he discovered that Uncle Edward had brought him a bone. There was also a gift for Susie—a pretty stuffed animal that even looked a little bit like Skippy.

But there was also a package for Peter in his uncle's large black suitcase. Father, Mother, Susie, and Skippy—everyone stood around Peter and peeked curiously over his shoulder. Peter unwrapped his present as fast as he could. "It's a camera!" he shouted with joy, "A camera!"

Yes, it was a real camera.

Susie also had a small camera, but hers was only a toy. She couldn't take pictures with it. She could only pretend. But Peter now had a real camera, with film, and even a few magicubes to insert for flash pictures. He was so excited he could barely stand still. Too bad Uncle Edward had not arrived a little earlier. Peter could have taken pictures of Skippy covered with soapsuds or Susie and the puppy all full of coal dust when they came up from the basement. But that didn't matter. Peter knew he would have many other chances to take pictures of Skippy. Yes, that's exactly what he would do. He would take pictures of Skippy and Susie, and of Mom and Dad, also.

Best of all, he planned to take his camera along on the next class trip. But one thing still worried Peter: would he ever be able to take pictures—really good pictures? Uncle Edward noticed the thoughtful look on Peter's face. "Come now, my boy, what's troubling you?"

"Tell me, Uncle," Peter replied, "won't picture-taking be too hard for me? When I think of Mr. Kraus, my teacher, and of all the dials he must set on his camera!"

Uncle Edward tried to reassure Peter: "Oh, no. You must not worry about that. Taking pictures is not difficult, especially not with this camera. This is a *Kodak Instamatic*® camera. It was especially designed to make picture-taking as easy as possible."

"You know, Uncle," said Peter feeling more confident, "if you will please put the film in the camera now, I can see how it is done!"

"Be glad to. First I must open the back cover of the camera. Then I simply place the film cartridge inside and just close the cover again. Now all I have to do is push this little lever called the 'film advance' with my thumb until it won't move any further. In the back window of the camera, the number "1" will appear."

"And now when I press the button on top, does that take a picture?"

"Yes, Peter, when you press this button you will get a photograph of whatever you see through the viewfinder."

"But what do I have to do if I want to take another picture?"

"You can take 12 snapshots with this film. Just move the film advance until it locks, and the camera will be ready for the next picture."

"Aha," said Peter, "now I understand. I'll go out in the street and take a photograph of Skippy."

"Go ahead," smiled his mother, "and take Susie along."

Peter and Susie ran down the stairs together.

Now the big moment had arrived when Peter would take his very first picture. He looked through the viewfinder and aimed at Skippy. To make his puppy turn out as large as possible in the photograph, Peter had to come a little closer to Skippy—about five feet away. He pressed the button—click—the first picture was taken. He worked the film advance with his thumb. At the same time, he took a step forward so that he was now only four feet away from Skippy. Click — there went the second picture. Twice Peter had aimed at the same target. Actually such targets are called "subjects" by real photog-

raphers. Both times Peter had stood close to his subject. He did this for a good reason. During his last vacation at the seashore, he had seen many people taking pictures of their families near beach umbrellas or sand castles, but they usually took these photographs from quite a distance away.

"That's something! It's hard to believe!" his father had said as he watched them. "People will turn out looking so small in the picture that they will be hard to recognize. Some photographers!"

Peter did not want to make the same mistake. That is why he now took a picture of Susie from about five feet away. Click—that's picture number 3.

"Where did you get that nice camera, Peter?" said a deep voice behind him.

Surprised, Peter turned around.

"Great-grandpa!" Susie threw her arms around her great-grandfather's neck. "Uncle Edward gave Peter that camera!"

"Well, well, Peter—are you going to take a picture of me too?"

"I would like to," said Peter. "Stand over here near the wall in front of the window, and I will take one right now." Click—that was picture number 4. Great-grandfather laughed, but he wasn't completely happy. "Peter, I don't think this picture of me will turn out very well. Look! I am standing right in front of a window with flowers on the sill. When people look at the picture, they will think that geraniums are growing out of my ears."

Peter wanted to try again: "Let's take another picture with the sky as background." No sooner said than done—click—picture number 5 was taken. "But tell me, Great-grandpa, how come you know so much about photography? Have you taken many pictures?"

"I certainly have, Peter! When I was younger I used to take a lot of pictures. But in those days, it was much more difficult than it is today. I have an idea, children: come and visit me this afternoon. Then I will show you the camera that I once used to take pictures."

Great-grandfather tells a story

Promptly at three o'clock, Peter and Susie arrived at Great-grandfather's house. From a large chest, he removed a strange object. It looked a little like an old broken-down accordion.

"This," he said, "was my first camera."

"Wow," exclaimed Peter, "that certainly is something to see! You have to be as strong as an elephant just to hold it."

"Oh, no, naturally I wasn't able to hold the camera. In those days, photography was not so easy as it is today. You couldn't just take a camera out of your pocket and press the button. The film had to be exposed for several seconds. If I had to hold the camera in my hand that long, all the pictures would be blurred. To support the camera, we had to use a heavy wooden stand called a 'tripod.'

"That was the only way the pictures on this wall could have turned out so sharp. I took them myself," said Great-grandfather with noticeable pride.

"Tell me," asked Susie, "what city were you in when you took this picture?"

Great-grandpa had to laugh: "This one? That's Maple Street where you live."

"Really?" Peter wondered out loud. "I wouldn't have recognized it. It looks so different today! And that one of the beautiful forest, where was that taken?"

"Oh, yes, the forest! It no longer exists. In its place stands the town of Dixville."

"That's where the new apartment buildings were built, isn't it?" asked Susie.

"Yes, that's right! When I was your age, there was such a large forest there that you could easily get lost in it. Deer used to scamper around among the trees. My grandfather told me that once even bears roamed there too."

"Did your grandfather also take pictures?" asked Susie.

"Oh, no, silly, they didn't have cameras in those days," interrupted Peter.

"Hold on a minute, now!" said Great-grandpa. "When my grandfather was exactly as small as you are, in the year 1839, almost one-and-a-half centuries ago, photography was invented. My grandfather himself wasn't able to take pictures yet, but once he had his own photograph taken. It was even more difficult to take a picture in those days than it was when I was a boy.

"There were no camera stores where you could buy film and have it processed. If you wanted to take a picture, you had to make your own photographic plates.

"The photographer could not store these plates and use them as he needed them. The plates were only usable while they were still wet. Therefore, he had to prepare a plate each time he wanted to take a photograph."

"You keep talking about plates," interrupted Peter, "but today we have film!"

"That's right, Peter. In the old days, they really did use glass plates coated with a layer of liquid called 'photographic emulsion.' Each time a person wanted to take a picture, he had to prepare one of these wet plates himself. Then, about 100 years ago, in 1871, the dry plate was invented.

"That was great progress! Plates for photographers could then be made in factories and stored for longer periods of time. Unfortunately, each plate could be used for only a single picture, and a new one had to be used for each photograph. Furthermore, these plates were quite heavy. Just imagine: Once, when a photographer wanted to take pictures in the Rocky Mountains, he had to load up four packmules—one with the camera and three with plates. On the return trip, a shepherd's dog who became startled by the caravan attacked the mules. The animals were frightened and ran off stumbling through rocks and underbrush. As a result, all the photographic plates ended up as a pile of glass splinters. The entire trip was wasted. Eighteen years after the invention of the dry plate, in 1889, another invention did away with all of these problems: George Eastman invented film. He also founded the Eastman Kodak Company which makes the camera and film you are using. Today, if necessary, you can take 12 or 20 pictures on your film without having to pause more than a moment between them.

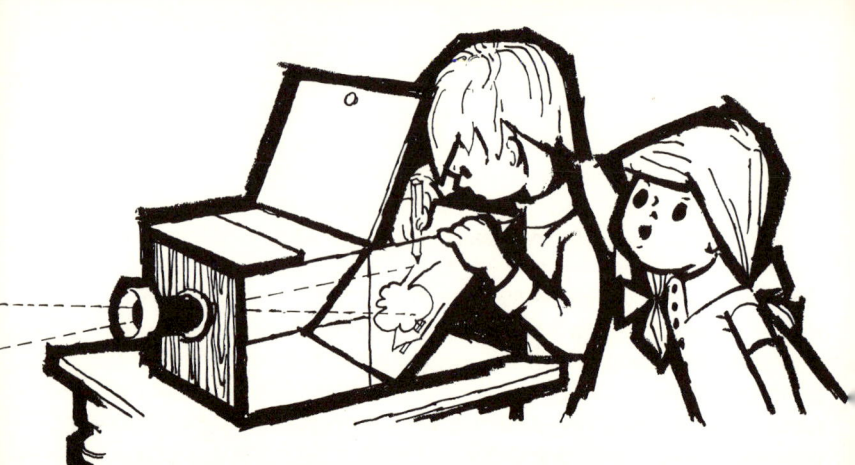

"With only a single hand movement you can advance the film in your *Instamatic* camera. If the old photographers had only known how simple photography would be some day! By the way, Peter, how long do you think the first photograph had to be exposed?"

"Well, I think probably very long, a minute, perhaps, or even two?"

"Wrong, my boy! Nicéphore Niepce made the first pictures around 1825. To do so, he had to expose them for eight full hours! Imagine, he would have had to expose his picture from ten in the morning to six in the evening! The shutter in your *Instamatic* camera opens for only 1/45th of a second when you use flash. It is hard to imagine a period of time as short as that. But when you use your camera for outdoor pictures with the sun shining, your exposures are even shorter—only 1/90th of a second! Figure it out for yourself: when photography was invented, the photographer had to expose two million, five hundred and ninety-two thousand times as long as you do now.

"But exposure times soon became much shorter—somewhere between 10 and 20 minutes. Even so, it was still not possible to photograph your dog Skippy in those days, and people had to remain completely motionless in front of the camera. That's why my grandfather had his picture taken only once and never again. His neck was sore for days afterwards."

"Now you're teasing us! How can anybody get a pain in the neck from photography?"

"Very simple! To keep my grandfather from moving during the exposure, the photographer had to place an iron support behind his neck and under his arms. Grandfather had to put up with this torture for 20 minutes. It was quite an ordeal!"

"This Mr. Niepce, the man you mentioned before," inquired Peter, "did he build the first camera?"

"Oh no, he made the first materials which were sensitive to light. Cameras were already invented. Although photographic cameras have been in existence for only 150 years, the camera itself is much, much older. Believe it or not, my grandfather's grandfather already owned a camera. By the way, it should still be around here someplace."

Great-grandfather took a large wooden box out of the chest. This box was much larger than his old camera. But it had a lens on the front, and it looked more or less as we might expect an old camera to look.

"That just doesn't make sense," mumbled Peter in amazement. "How is that possible? A camera at a time when photographs were not even invented! What would anyone do with a thing like that? Without film, wasn't a camera completely useless?"

"It wasn't quite as useless as you might think," responded Great-grandfather. "In those days, cameras were used as tools for drawing."

"Drawing!" Peter and Susie exclaimed together.

"Yes, for drawing. Let me show you." Great-grandpa put a piece of paper in the drawing camera and placed the camera on a table near the window.

"You can see the house across the street and the trees," exclaimed Susie with surprise, "but they are all upside down!"

"Can I try drawing on it?" asked Peter as he fumbled in his pocket for a pencil.

"Of course," said Great-grandpa, "try it!"

"It really works!" said the boy.

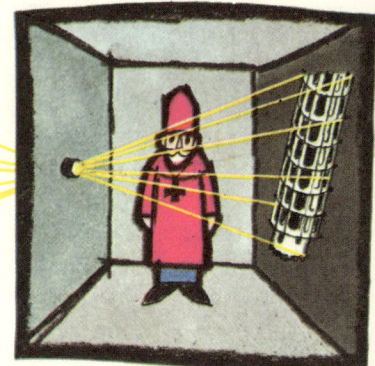

"That's right," replied Great-grandpa. "Anyone can draw with this machine."

"This is really terrific! Who invented it?"

"I'll be glad to tell you: On a beautiful day long ago, the famous Arab wise man, Alhazen of Basra, was sitting in his tent. He was just taking a little rest during a tiring journey across the desert. He was enjoying his water pipe and puffing white clouds of smoke into the air. His tent had a small hole on one side. This was quite understandable. The trips with camels across the desert lasted for weeks and many things wore out. But Alhazen suddenly observed something strange. The light rays coming through that hole were forming a light spot on the opposite wall of the tent. In the light spot something seemed to be moving. Alhazen looked a little closer. The figure of a camel was moving in that spot—an upside-down camel! 'By the beard of the prophet!' Alhazen was puzzled. Camels don't ordinarily stand on their heads—especially not his favorite camel. He just had to understand the reason for this strange occurrence.

"A picture of his favorite camel, who was tied up outside, really was coming through the hole onto the wall of his tent. And so it came about that Alhazen discovered the first camera known to man. The word 'camera' means nothing more than 'chamber.' Later on, the Arabic wise man purposely built chambers with small holes in order to observe the sun without being blinded by it.

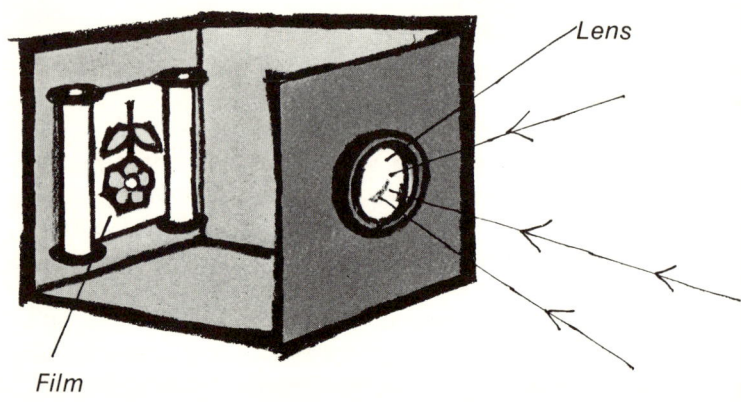

Lens

Film

"But the thought of tracing these images onto paper did not occur to him. He was a Mohammedan, and his religion did not allow him to draw people, animals, or landscapes.

"Six-hundred years later, the Italians discovered that such a dark chamber with a hole in the wall could be used for drawing. They called this device, 'camera obscura'—dark chamber.

"It would have been boring to draw the same landscape over and over, so they built chambers in the form of tents or small wooden huts that could be taken apart and moved from place to place on mules or horses. Finally, someone thought of building a small wooden box with a hole on one side and a piece of paper on the other. That was how the drawing camera was invented."

Peter was still thinking about the hole. "Then we really don't need a lens for taking a picture. A simple hole will do just as well. If we darken this room leaving only a hole, would we then see the street outside on this wall?"

"We certainly would," said Great-grandpa. "How would you like to try it? It's more fun to do than talk about."

By using black paper, the three of them were able to darken the room completely. Then Great-grandpa poked a small hole through the paper, and behold: the house and trees from across the street appeared on the wall, and they were standing on their heads!

To explain to Peter and Susie just how a small hole could produce such a miracle, Great-grandpa used colored pencils to make some diagrams. First he drew a colorful parrot with a red head, blue wings, and yellow feet. "Whoops," he said, "I almost forgot to draw the most important thing: the sun that shines on our parrot. There, that's better. It sends a ray of light to the head of the bird, but the light beam bounces off the feathers like a rubber ball. As it does, the light ray changes slightly. It becomes weaker, and also takes on a red color. Here we have a chamber with a hole. The light beam passes through the hole. Because every light ray travels exactly in a straight line, we can tell precisely where it will hit the wall. Coming from the head of our parrot, it travels through the hole and arrives at the bottom of the wall. At the same time, the sun sends a light ray to the yellow feet of the parrot. This light is bounced back in yellow and passes through the hole. Having come from below, it will hit the wall at the top. A light ray cast by the sun on the wings bounces off blue, and after passing through the hole, will arrive more or less in the middle of the wall.

"So you see, by knowing that light rays travel in a straight line, we can trace their paths and understand why a small hole can produce a picture and why the picture will be upside-down."

There was still one point that Peter could not understand: "Why must the hole be small to produce a picture? Why isn't there a picture on the wall when we open the window? Light rays come through the window too, lots of them. Can you explain that to us?"

"I'll do better than that; I'll show you."

As he spoke, Great-grandpa poked a few more holes into the black paper that was covering the window.

A second, a third, and a fourth light spot appeared on the wall, each with an upside-down view of the scenery outside. Soon the wall became too small to contain all the pictures that appeared on it. The light spots began to overlap. The pictures gradually became unclear, paler, blurred, and more indistinguishable. Finally they merged into overall whiteness. No picture could be recognized any more.

"Okay, I understand," said Peter, "you don't have to make so many holes in the paper that nothing is left of the picture! But why does a camera need a lens when a simple hole will produce a picture?"

"That's easy to explain," said Great-grandpa, pleased that Peter was so interested.

"You can also take photographs with a box that only has a hole in it. But the hole has to be so small that only a little light can go through. Therefore, you would have to expose the picture for a long time. But we could use a much larger hole if we put a lens in front of it. This was already done 400 years ago with drawing cameras. The lenses on today's cameras, however, are usually complicated devices made up of several lenses put together."

"Well, now I understand the whole thing. The first camera with a lens is about 400 years old."

"Wrong," smiled Great-grandpa, "it is several hundred million years old!

"Don't look so confused, Peter! It wasn't man who invented the camera with a lens, it was nature."

Peter suddenly caught on. "The eye, of course, the eye, that's it!"

"Right! The eye gathers individual light rays with a lens and casts a picture on the inside of the eye. If our eyes were not able to sort out individual light rays in order to form a picture, we wouldn't be able to see," confirmed Great-grandpa. He continued: "The eyes of fish are the oldest cameras with lenses. Lizards and snakes, birds and four-legged animals have eyes that are very similar to fish eyes. But nature once also used a pinhole camera with a lens: The octopus in our oceans has eyes with an open hole—a regular pinhole camera. This creature has been swimming in our seas since the beginning of time: long before man, long before the birds, even long before there were fish. Nature did what man did: it first tried out the pinhole camera eye and then created the eye with a lens. The eye with a lens that many other living creatures have in addition to man and fish is quite similar to the camera that Uncle Edward gave you."

As Great-grandpa explained all this to the children, they were as excited as if he were telling them a thrilling adventure story.

Lens
Iris
Lid
Eyeball
Retina

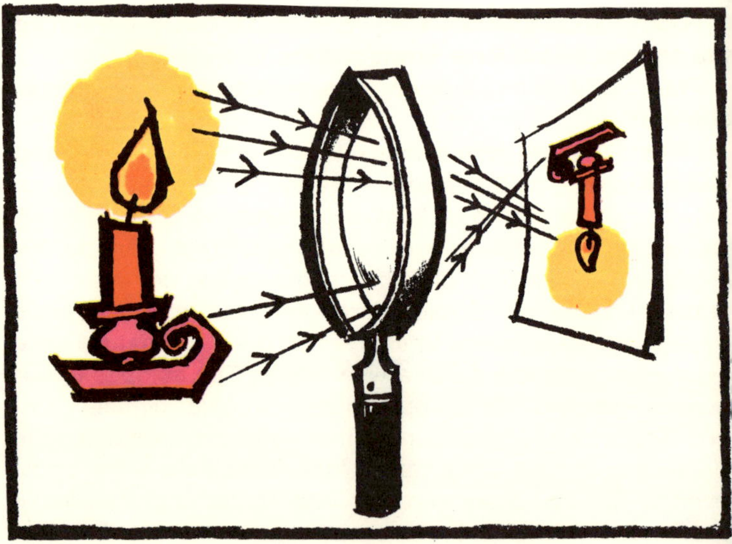

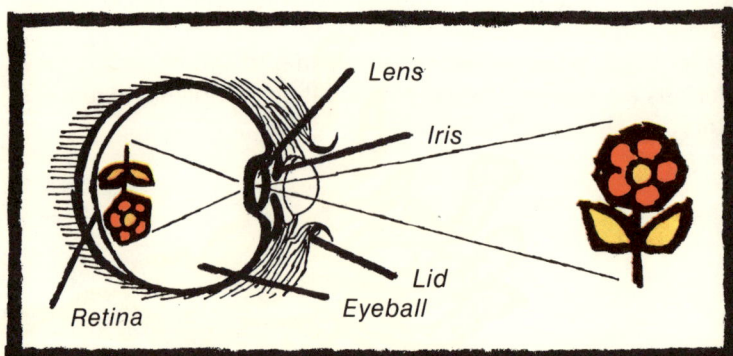

Finally, Great-grandpa said: "Enough for today! Peter, can you tell me when Uncle Edward plans to leave?"

"Yes," said Peter, "I believe he will be leaving tomorrow afternoon."

"Then I'd better take you home now. I want to make sure that I do not miss him."

Peter takes his uncle to the train

Right after lunch the next day, Peter accompanied his uncle to the train station. Naturally, he took along his camera so he could take a picture of Uncle Edward before he left.

Uncle Edward huffed and puffed trying to get his suitcase up the small but steep hill to the railroad station. You could see by the look on his face that it wasn't an easy job. At that moment, Peter pressed the button on his camera.

"We had better hurry, or I'll miss my train!" said Uncle Edward. Had he only known what the clerk would tell him ten minutes later, he wouldn't have been in such a hurry. "No, sir, there is no train leaving for Earlsville at 2:43 p.m. That is the time when the train is due to *arrive* from Earlsville!"

Uncle Edward had misread the train schedule. How could he have made such a mistake! Fortunately, another train was scheduled to leave in an hour and a half, and Uncle Edward's good spirits returned when he heard this. "You know what? We will go to the waiting room. You can have some lemonade and I'll get myself something to drink also."

They had just taken their first sip when a ray of sunlight made their glasses sparkle. This reminded Peter of a question he had been meaning to ask his uncle: "Please tell me, Uncle, how do the light rays form a picture on the film?"

"I'll be glad to explain that to you, my boy.

"First you should know that a little ray of light may appear dainty and delicate, but it is actually quite a strong thing. Look out this window! Why do you suppose that Weber's clothing store has an awning over the display window?"

"I guess," said Peter, "so that the shoppers who stand in front of it don't become sunburned."

"That might be one of the effects of the sunlight," laughed Uncle Edward, "but that isn't the reason. When light is allowed to shine on fabric for a long time, the colors begin to fade. Not only does this happen with fabric, but it also happens with paper and many other things.

"If I place a pair of scissors on a piece of red paper and leave them in the sun for a couple of weeks, where would the red gradually fade?"

"Everywhere except under the scissors?" guessed Peter.

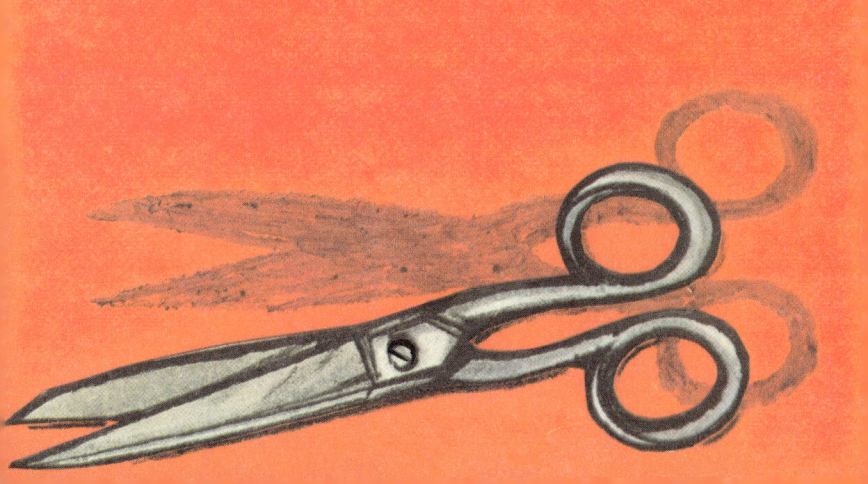

"That's right! The paper exposed to the sunlight would turn light red leaving a dark red silhouette of the scissors under it. That is actually a form of photography," said the uncle. "But it doesn't take weeks with film because a picture is formed in only 1/90th of a second, and for good reason! On the colored paper, the light rays produce the picture directly. This process takes a long time! Film, however, is coated with a layer of emulsion that contains silver. This emulsion has very special qualities. When you have taken your snapshot, the picture cannot be seen right away on the film. It only appears when the film is developed. This happens when the film is dipped into two solutions: first a liquid developer and then a fixing bath. In other words, the light only prepares the film so that these solutions will make the picture appear. Because of the emulsion, light rays need only a very short time to act on the film. Those portions of the film that were exposed to no light or very little light become clear and transparent when bathed in these solutions. Those areas which were exposed to more light, however, form black images consisting of very tiny silver grains. So you see, darkness forms clear, transparent areas, and light produces black areas.

"The picture on the film actually shows the world in reverse. A black horse appears white; a snowman looks like he has been covered with mud."

"In other words," said Peter, thinking out loud, "if I had photographed my dog Skippy after we brought him up from the coal cellar, he would have turned out snow white on the film."

"That's right, Peter! These pictures in reverse are called 'negatives!' It doesn't matter that the shadows are bright and that the sunny areas appear dark because the prints made from these negatives will turn out right. On them, the snowman will be white again and the black horse will be as black as he should be."

Peter was sorry to interrupt: "Too bad, Uncle, I could listen to you for hours, but you must be careful not to miss your train!"

The station master had already signaled the departure of the train when Uncle Edward handed some money to Peter through the train window.

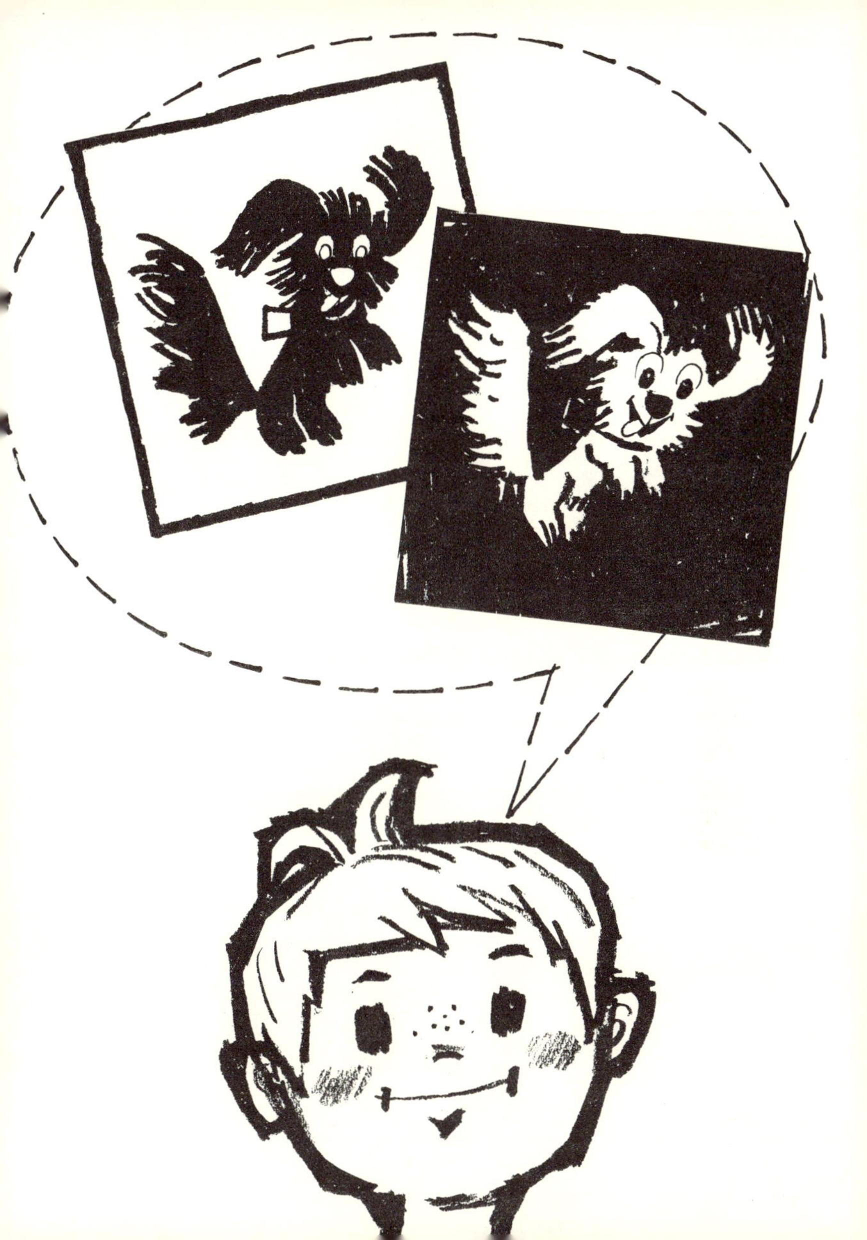

"Here, Peter, this is to pay for having your film processed."

"Oh, thank you, Uncle Edward! Many, many thanks for everything!"

Slowly, the train began to move. Almost at the exact same time, a cross-country express train arrived at the next platform.

Chasing an astronaut with Reporter Kelly

Strange, the cross-country express usually passed right through the station without stopping! Peter ran down the stairs to the underpass trying to reach the other platform. But he couldn't make his way through a crowd of people all surging toward the exit door. Instead, he was carried along by the crowd of pushing and shoving people.

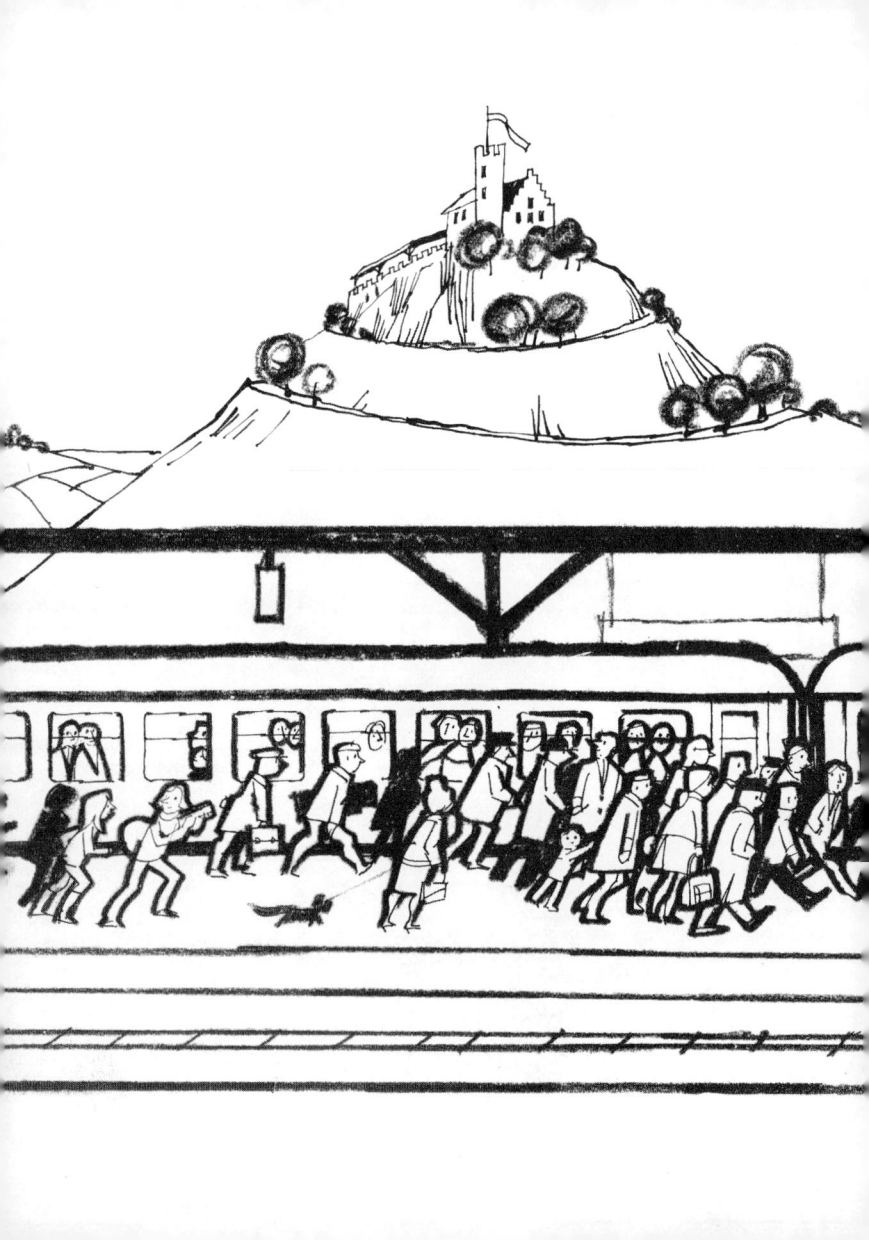

This must be what it feels like to be a sardine in a can! Peter strained his neck trying to see what all the commotion was about. Funny, that man right in the center of the crowd, how familiar he looked! But from where? Where could he have seen him before? On television—yes, that was it! He had seen him on the news program, except that then he was wearing an unusual helmet which had made him hard to recognize. It

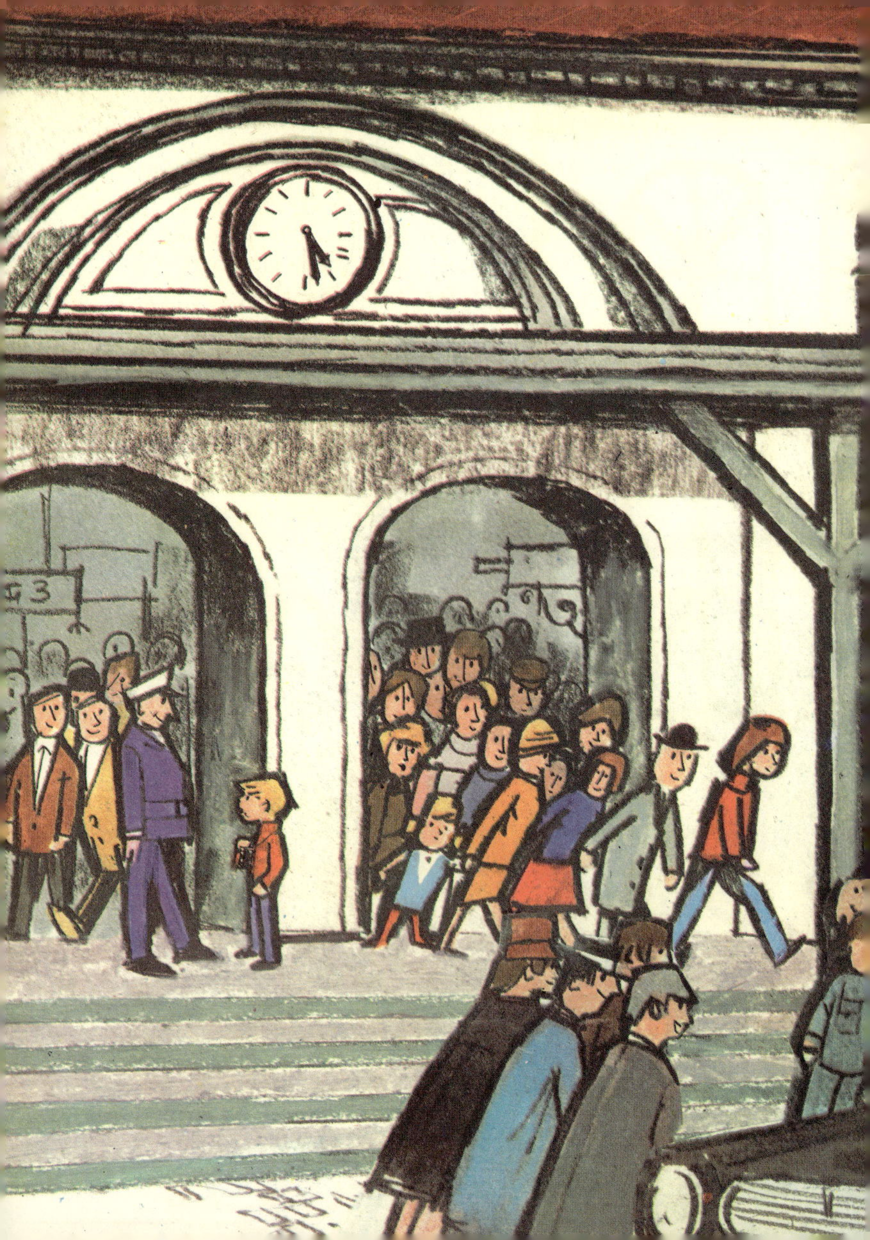

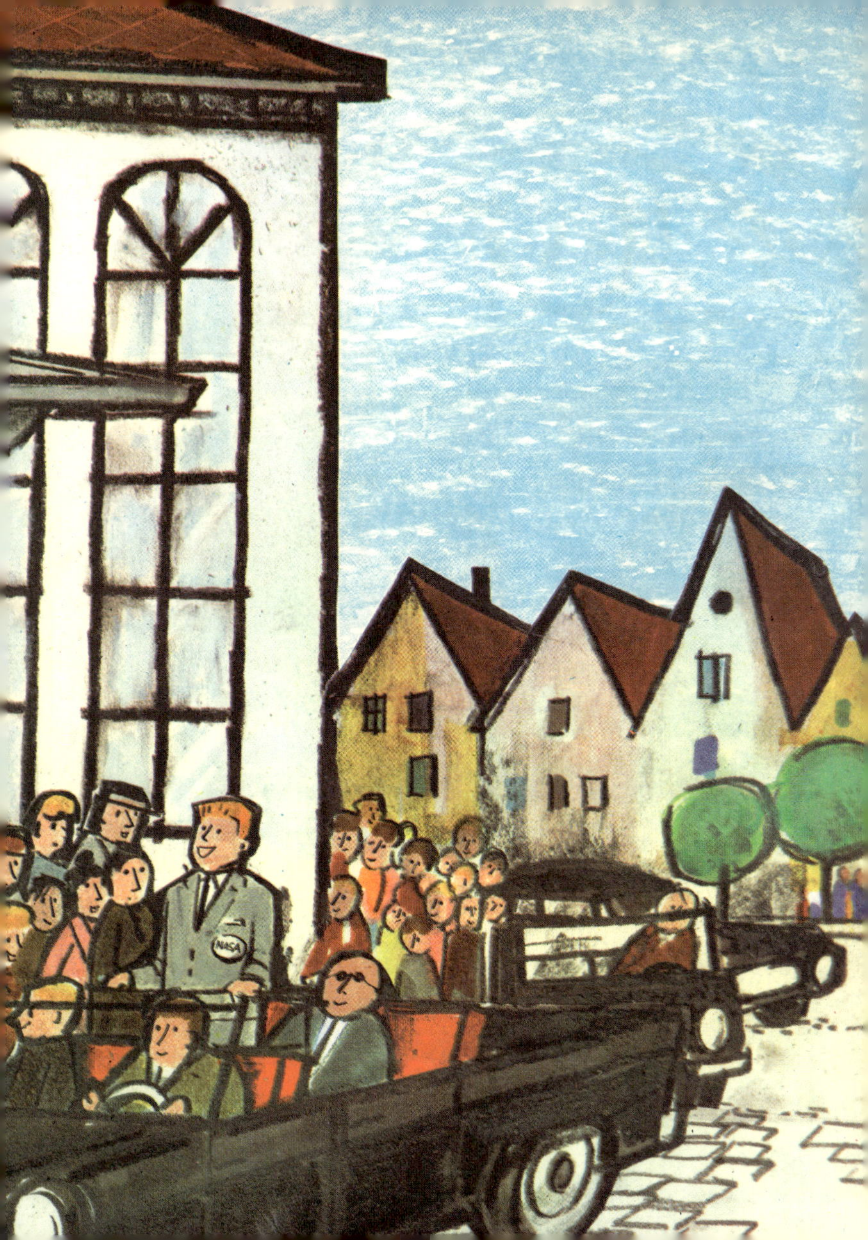
NASA

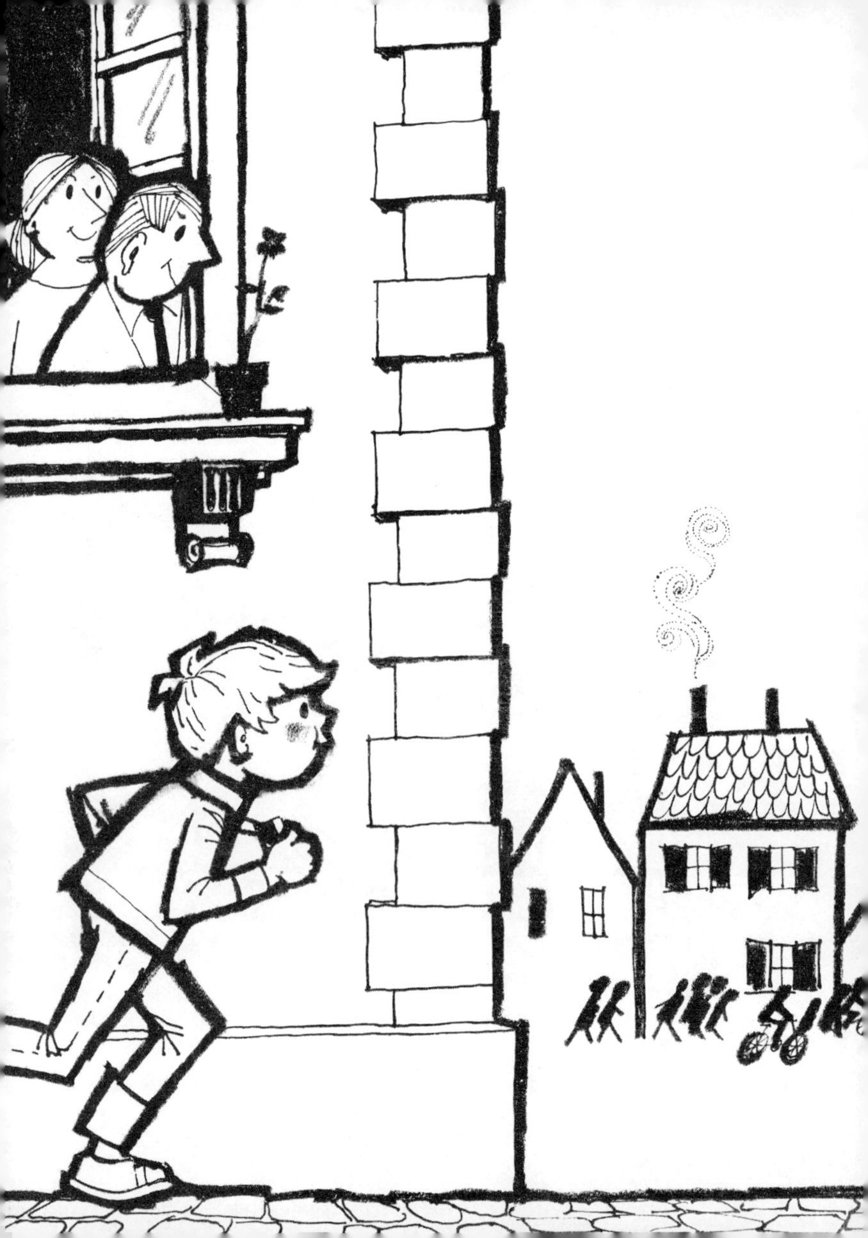

was the famous astronaut, Astronaut McLunic. Unfortunately, Peter wasn't able to get any closer to the space traveler. In fact, he was gradually being pushed away. McLunic was just getting into a waiting car as Peter managed to squeeze out of the station building. His car was the first in a long line of black and important looking limousines.

A policeman told Peter that the astronaut was being taken to a reception at City Hall. Without a moment's thought, Peter set off at a run toward City Hall.

A large crowd had already gathered there. Everyone wanted to see McLunic, and many people had cameras. Peter squeezed through the crowd until he got to a tall man holding a camera with an unusually long lens. He just had to be a reporter.

"Excuse me, please, Mr. . . . ."

"Kelly, my name is Kelly!" said the reporter, completing Peter's sentence. "You are probably curious about my camera aren't you? And right you are! It is a rather special camera. You can change the lenses on it!"

Peter was impressed: "Change lenses! But what for?"

"Well, look, there are so many people gathered here that I can't get everyone into the picture with my regular lens. That's why I have to switch to a so-called 'wide-angle lens.' Although it will make the people look smaller in the picture, it will let me get nearly twice as many people into the photograph. That way I can show what a really large crowd of people has gathered here."

45

Peter was curious: "Is that a wide-angle lens on your camera now?"

CITY HALL

"No, this is a telephoto lens. It does the same thing for the camera as binoculars do for your eyes. It makes things look much closer. I can photograph McLunic from way back here and still make him appear large on the picture. With your camera, you have to get all the way to the front of the crowd if you want to get a good picture of McLunic!"

"With such a long lens I could photograph wild animals without disturbing them. Or I could take pictures of a circus from the cheapest seat way in the back. That's great! When I get bigger and earn some money, I'm going to buy myself a lens like that. Do you always use that camera?"

"No, I don't! Sometimes I borrow a camera from my brother. He is a professional photographer with his own studio. When I need to, I borrow his large camera."

"Large camera? My great-grandfather showed me a large camera that he once used for taking pictures."

"That's right, today's large camera still looks a little like the cameras of long ago. But it only looks that way. These cameras are actually very modern, and they take pictures that are larger than a page in your school notebook. When you see the large pictures on advertising posters, remember that they were made with such big cameras."

Peter was somewhat confused: "But I thought I could take large pictures with my camera too?"

"You can. Your photo dealer can make postcard-size enlargements from your film, or even bigger sizes. But large cameras have even larger negatives. And these can be blown up sometimes to pictures of six to ten feet in height. Of course, it isn't very easy to handle such a complicated camera. But we had better pay attention! Something seems to be happening up ahead!" Peter ducked between the legs of the man in front of him. He wriggled his way forward towards the entrance of City Hall. A man tried to keep him back! "Hold it, kid! Don't be so pushy!"

Out of breath and red in the face, Peter finally reached the steps of the building. He arrived not a second too soon. Astronaut McLunic was just stepping through the entryway. Peter yanked his camera up. As the astronaut began waving to the crowd, Peter pressed down on the button and quickly advanced the film. Click—another picture! Once again, press and release. He followed close at the astronaut's heels. Squeezing past him, he got a picture from the front; click, advance the film, click, and . . . . It all happened much faster than can be described here. Peter knew that he had to take as many snapshots as he possibly could. In the excitement, one or two might not turn out. If he took four or five pictures, he had a better chance of having at least a few lively shots in all the commotion. He still had two pictures left on the film. Just then a tall man moved in front of him. How annoying! But Peter didn't give up. Since he couldn't see anything through the veiwfinder, he stretched his arms and held the camera above the crowd, aiming more or less at where McLunic should be.

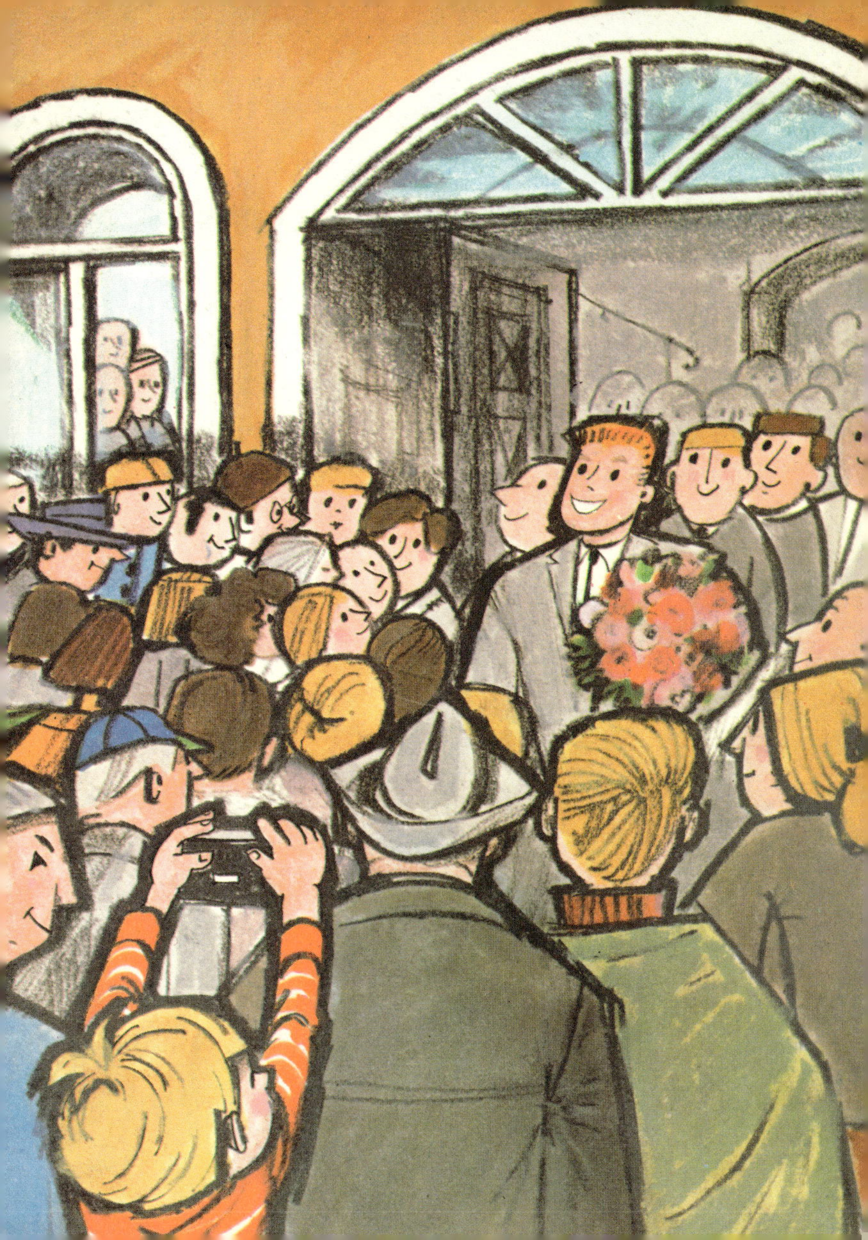

Click—I hope that was right, thought Peter. He squeezed his way back through the crowd. Relieved to be breathing freely again, he ran back to Reporter Kelly. How clever that Kelly! He simply climbed into a tree and aimed at the astronaut with his long lens. Then all he had to do was wait like a hunter in his lookout.

This is an interesting picture too, thought Peter, and click—Reporter Kelly was captured on Peter's film. The first cartridge was finished. He could hardly wait to get to Reddy's Camera Store to have the film developed.

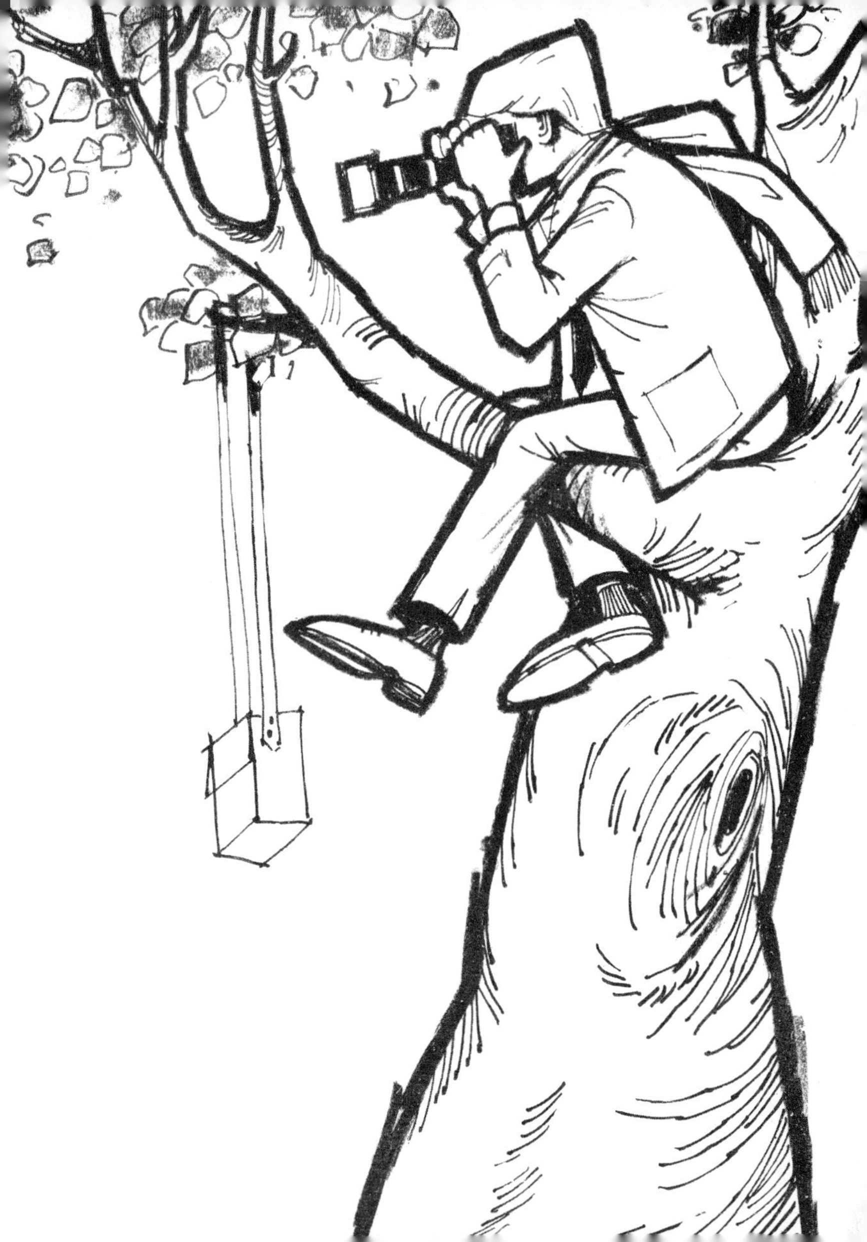

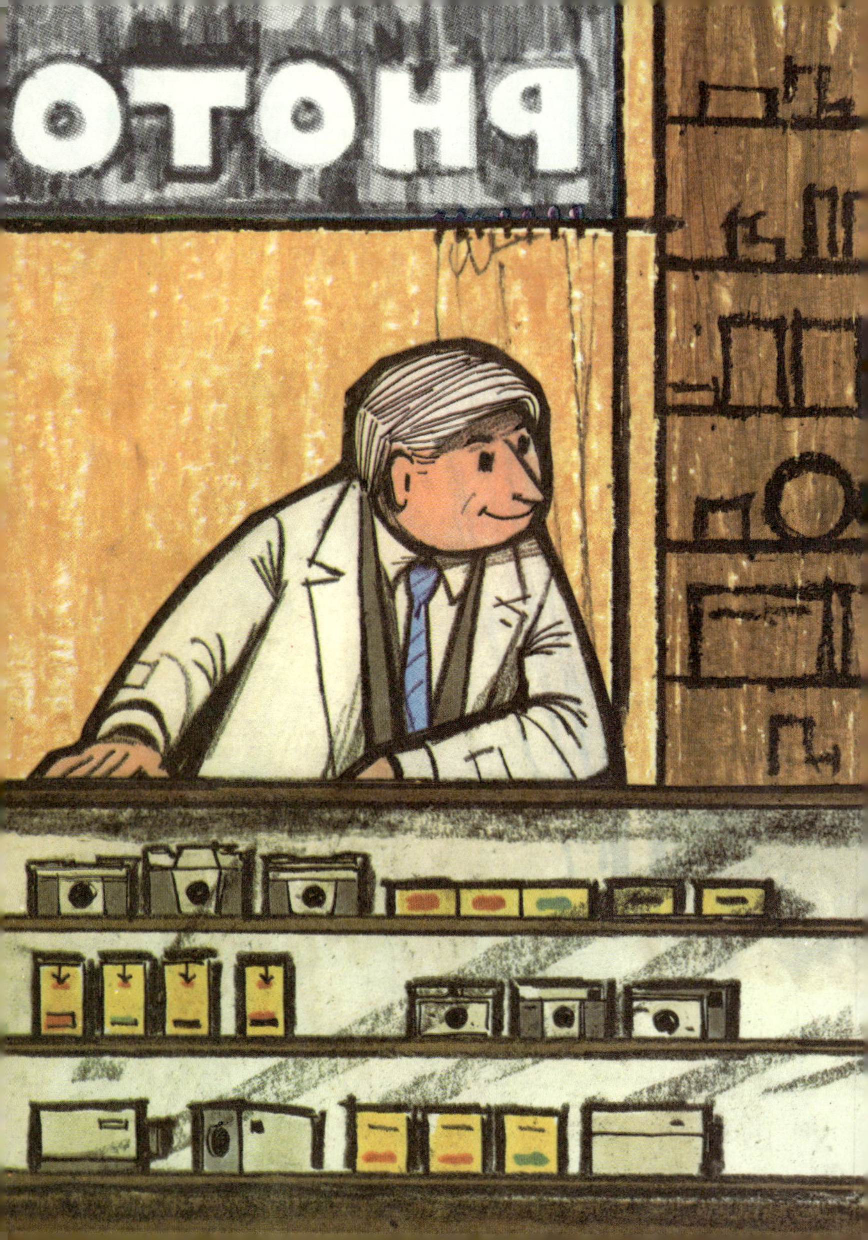
PHOTO

At the camera store

In the store, Peter pushed the film-advance lever until it stopped. Then he opened the back of his *Instamatic* camera, removed the film, and handed it to the clerk. "Please develop my film and make a print of each picture, Mr. Reddy. When can I pick them up?"

"Tomorrow afternoon, Peter," Mr. Reddy replied. "Would you like to buy another film cartridge now?"

Peter bought new film so he could continue taking pictures without delay.

"Do you want me to load it for you?" asked Mr. Reddy.

"Oh, no, I can do that myself," said Peter, a little hurt that Mr. Reddy didn't think that he could load his *Instamatic* camera himself. He tore open the package, placed the cartridge in the camera, closed the cover, and advanced the film until it stopped.

Back home again, Peter attached a magicube onto his camera. Then he opened the kitchen door just as his mother was pushing a delicious cake into the oven.

"Mom, look over here!" said Peter, and the moment she turned, the flash went off.

In the living room, he placed himself about six feet away from his father who was just listening to the news: "Dad, don't look so serious! Smile!" Click! He wanted to take still another picture, but his father waved his hand at him and said, "That's enough, Peter! I want to listen to the news!" Click! Peter had already taken the picture. On the radio, the announcer was reviewing the events of the day, but Peter wasn't interested. Only one thought occupied his mind: how would the first pictures turn out when he picked them up tomorrow at the camera store?

The next morning seemed like it would never end according to Peter. At last, it was time to go to the camera store.

"I've got your pictures, Peter," said Mr. Reddy.

Now came the exciting moment! Peter held his very first pictures in his hand. There they were! There was Skippy just like in real life! The first two pictures that Peter had taken were of his little dog. The second which he took from only four feet away was even better than the first.

The third picture showed Susie. It had come out very well! But the two pictures of Great-grandfather were as different as day and night. To be truthful, one of the pictures was not very good—it really looked as though geraniums were growing out of Great-grandfather's ears! But the other picture with the sky as background was much better. The one of Uncle Edward came out well too. It really showed how hard he was struggling with his luggage. And now Peter turned to the five pictures that he had taken of Astronaut McLunic. Two of them were blurred. In the excitement, perhaps he hadn't held the camera completely still. But the other three pictures turned out quite well and sharp too. Peter was really proud of these pictures. But he had to laugh when he got to the picture of Reporter Kelly. How funny he looked sitting up in the tree! In fact, he looked much funnier in the picture than he did in real life.

Mr. Reddy liked the pictures too, particularly the shots of McLunic. "You really caught the astronaut very well, Peter! Especially this one! My compliments on an excellent snapshot! Think it over—you may want me to make an enlargement of it."

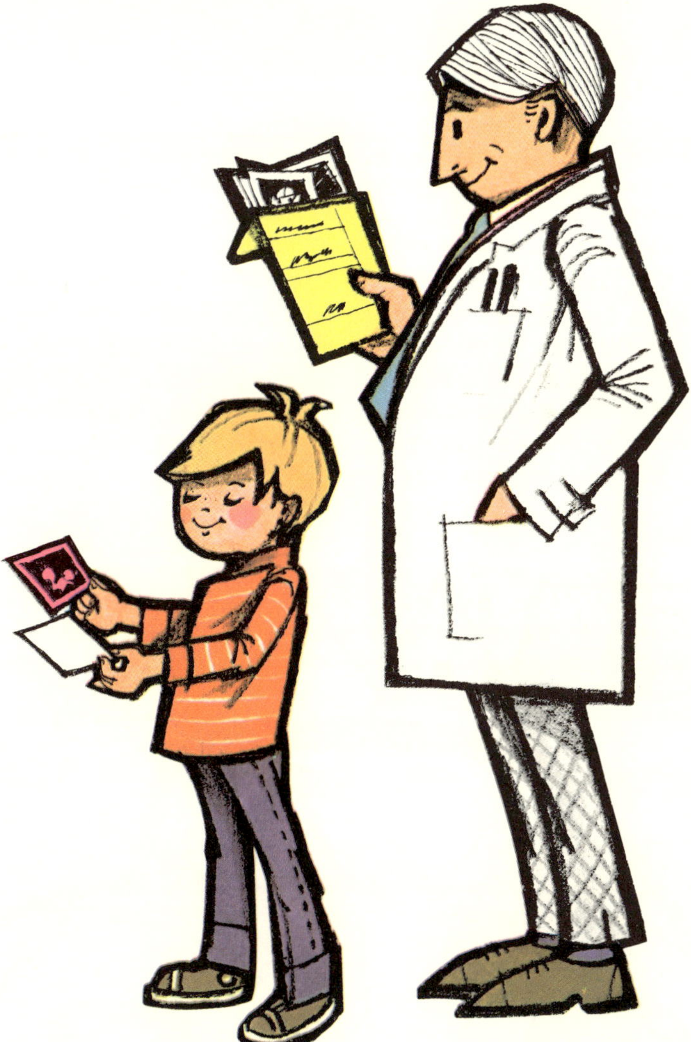

Peter helps the police

A heavy rain was falling as Peter stepped out of the camera store. It was coming down from the sky almost as if it were pouring from a faucet. Peter wasn't afraid of water, but it was raining so hard that he was very glad to see his father come by in his car. Peter quickly jumped in to keep from getting soaked.

"I still have another errand to run," said his father, "but I'll take you home first." As he spoke, he turned off his windshield wipers. The rain had stopped falling as suddenly as it had begun.

But Peter's father continued to drive very carefully. "When this winding road gets wet, it's as slippery as soap."

Peter didn't hear the last statement. His attention was focused on a car that was roaring toward them from a side street on the right. It was going at a terribly fast speed and signaling a left turn into the main traffic.

Peter had just enough time to wonder, "At that speed, I hope he has time enough to stop...." Crrunch! Bang! Metal crashed against metal! Brakes screeched loudly! The speed-

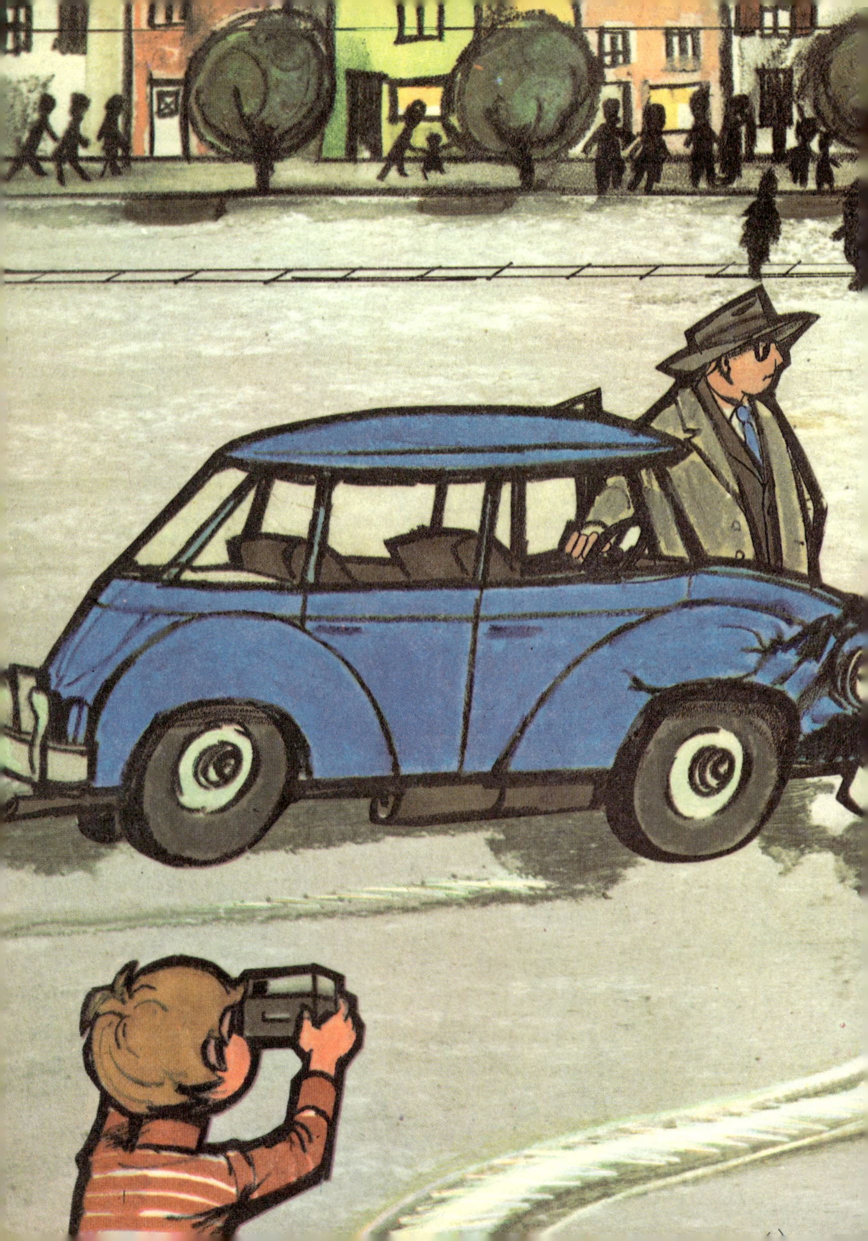

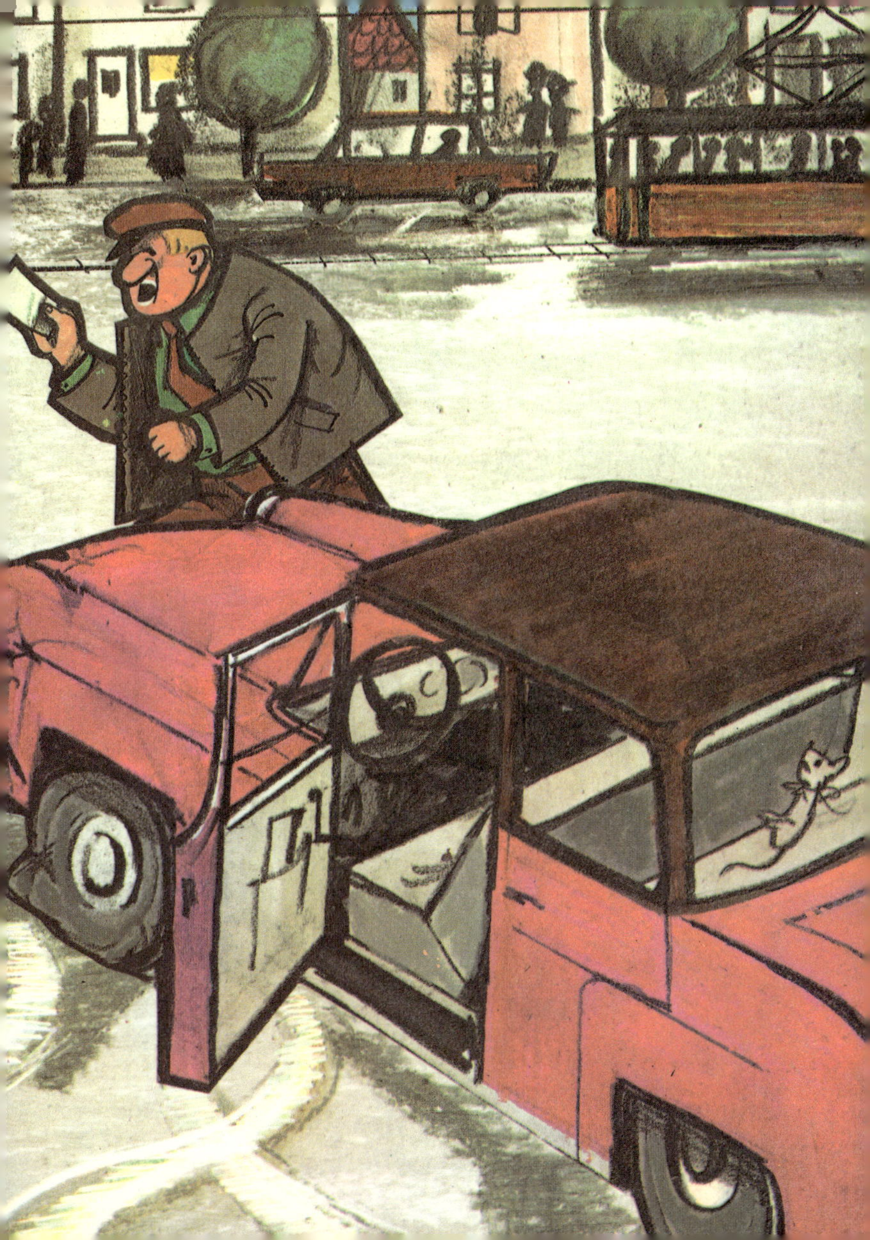

er's car had gone into a skid during his turn, and it crashed right into the front fender of his father's car. It then bounced back into the opposite lane.

For a few seconds, Peter and his father sat motionless. They were dazed but not hurt. The fender and the headlight of their car had been badly damaged. A real fender-bender! The speeder also appeared to be unharmed. In fact, he seemed to be in especially good form. He came over to them shouting, "Where'd you learn to drive—in a gardener's school? What made you turn left and hit my brand new car? Now it's ready for the scrap heap. You just wait—you're going to pay for this!"

Peter's father was so overwhelmed by all this bullying that at first he was speechless.

But Peter, who was not directly involved in the argument, was able to recover from his surprise more quickly. He took a picture of the bully standing threateningly in front of his father, holding a piece of paper under his nose and growling, "Now you write down here that this accident was your fault! Then we won't need the police, and it will be cheaper for you!"

At that moment, a few rays of sunshine peeked through an opening in the clouds making the wet pavement and the skid marks, in particular, glitter brightly. Peter noticed this and quickly advanced his film. He took a picture of the skid marks. Perhaps I could get a better view of them from the other side, thought Peter, and he moved over a few steps. Just as he thought! The skid marks were much clearer from this point because the sun was directly in the background. When he was standing with the sun behind him, the skid marks could hardly be seen. He quickly took a few more pictures of the wet pavement.

After a while, a crowd began to form. "Did anyone see the accident?" Peter's father was trying to find a witness who could testify that it was the bully and not he who had caused the accident. Although he repeated the question several times, nobody came forward. Could it really be true that no one had seen what happened? At last, one person volunteered to call the police. In the meantime, it had started to rain again.

Finally a patrol car arrived. Officer Fry filled out the accident report. First he questioned Mr. Boller—that was the name of the speeder. Peter took advantage of the opportunity by taking a picture of Officer Fry doing his job. Then it was his father's turn to describe what happened. The two descriptions didn't seem to agree! Therefore, Officer Fry tried to find a witness. No luck.

"Too bad the skid marks have been washed away by the rain, otherwise it would be easy to see who was at fault," said Officer Fry to another policeman.

At this point, Peter opened the back of his camera, took out the film cartridge, handed it to the officer, and said quite calmly: "Officer, I took some pictures of the skid marks when they were still visible."

"Good boy. If these photos turn out, you will have done us a big favor!" Officer Fry was as surprised as Peter's father, who had been too busy to notice what his son was doing.

All at once, the expression on the bully's face became quite meek. "Officer," he said, sounding almost polite, "if I can, I would like to add a few things to my earlier statement."

"Oh you would, would you? You had better come with me to the station. We will be pleased to listen to everything you have to say." Then the officer turned to Peter and his father: "It would be a good idea if you would come to see me tomorrow at the station at nine o'clock. In the meantime, I will have the pictures processed."

The next morning was a big success for Peter. Everyone was waiting for him and his father: Officer Fry, other members of the police force, and even Mr. Boller who could hardly be recognized. Yesterday, he had acted so big and bold. Now he was sitting quietly in the corner. The pictures had clearly shown that he alone was at fault. Now it was up to him to pay the damages.

Officer Fry sounded somewhat official as he made a short speech to Peter: "We must thank you for being so prompt in photographing the skid marks. How nice it would be if many more citizens would help us so well and so quickly. Assistance can be useful only if it is carried out properly. A witness to an accident or a crime should never step into the scene or try to take any action himself. That might easily destroy valuable clues. It is also dangerous to try to stop an escape. Criminals may be armed, and the person running away from a crime is often so frightened that he might react violently. Chasing a criminal as you've seen it done in the movies or on television is especially dangerous for a young boy. On the other hand, young people could be very helpful if they would carefully observe what happened or—if they do as you did—take a picture at the right time."

At this point, Officer Fry gave Peter the developed film. "The pictures of the skid marks turned out very well, especially those taken against the sun,." he explained to Peter, who looked at him with a surprised expression. "Pictures taken with the sun shining at you are more difficult to take."

The officer handed Mr. Boller the picture on which he appeared close up. It showed him big and pompous trying to intimidate Peter's father. Even though the photograph was quite good, Mr. Boller didn't seem to like it very much.

Peter's first flash pictures had also turned out well. The three snapshots were sharp and properly exposed. As we recall, Peter had first asked his mother and then his father to pose so that he could take the flash pictures. But Peter was surprised that the third picture turned out best of all, much better than the two posed pictures. His father was impatiently waving his hand and looking annoyed—an interesting and amusing picture. But now his father was by no means angry. Quite to the contrary, he had to laugh over the humorous picture.

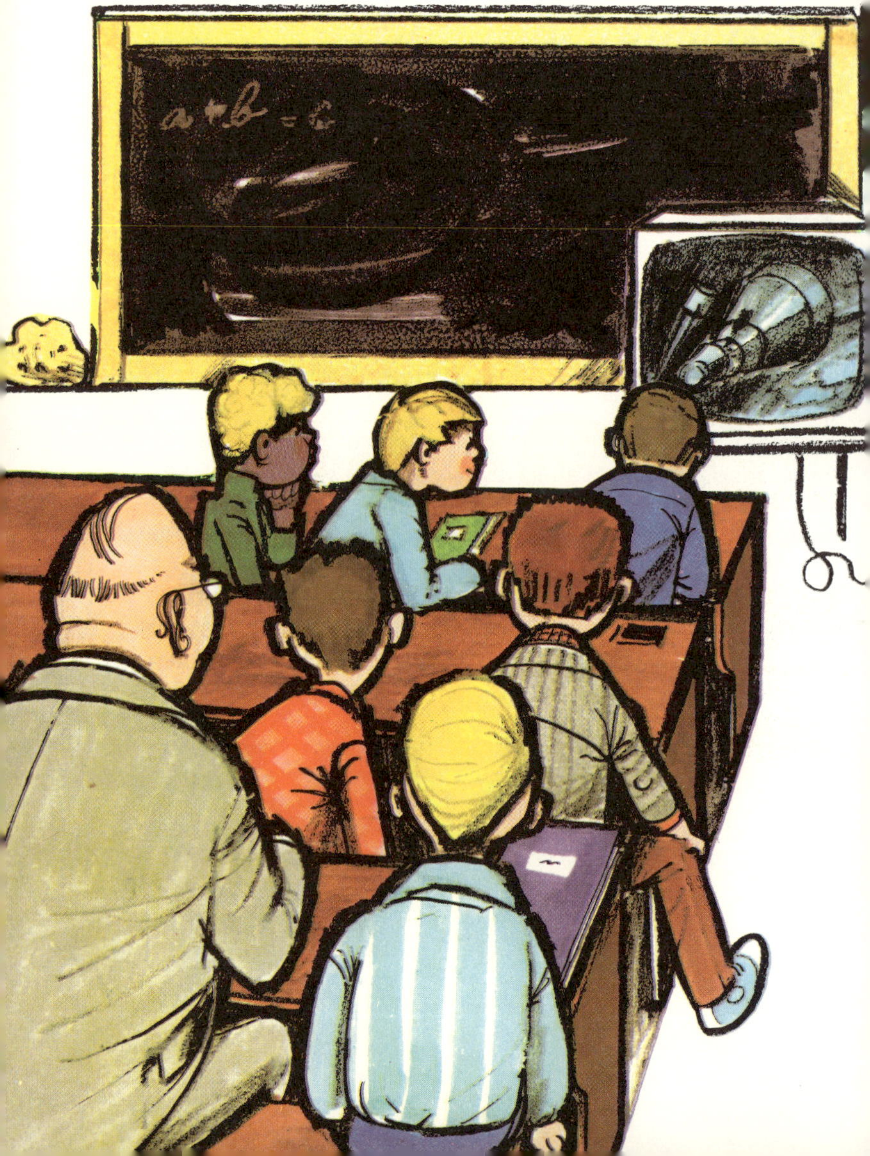
a+b=c

Photography in space

The next day, Peter's classroom looked different from the way it usually appeared. First Peter noticed that his teacher's desk was missing from the front of the room. Instead, Mr. Kraus was sitting at a pupil's desk way in the back. A large television set was placed on a stand where his desk used to be. The class was already watching a television broadcast from the capital city highlighting the reception for Astronaut McLunic. Just as Peter came in, the program was featuring a report of the astronaut's latest space flight.

The screen showed a movie which was made by McLunic's co-pilot out in space. The space capsule was circling the earth at an incredible speed. McLunic stepped out of the capsule and floated in space, attached to the capsule by only a thin cord. He raised a camera—and actually began to take pictures while floating free far above the earth. Then a few pictures were shown of the film he took during his space walk.

One of the pictures clearly showed the outline of South America. The next picture was of Africa and the Mediterranean. On the one of Europe, only Italy and Greece could be seen; the rest was hidden by clouds.

How impressive these pictures were! But the most remarkable one was the photograph showing the entire earth. It appeared on the screen as a round planet in the same way that we are used to seeing the sun or the moon.

Mr. Kraus turned off the TV set. "Now you have seen what Astronaut McLunic accomplished in space. He was here in town the day before yesterday. Perhaps some of you saw him?" A few of the students raised their hands; they had also been in front of City Hall on the day of his visit.

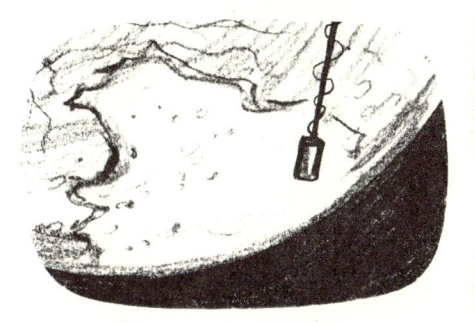

Tom and Tim, the twins in the class and two quite mischievous young boys, were very proud. They were able to get an autograph during McLunic's visit. Peter could no longer hold back his excitement. He proudly showed his snapshots. Everyone gathered around him to admire them.

"They are really good photographs," complimented the teacher. "Please make some prints for me. I have started an album of important space pictures in which I collect all newspaper clippings and pictures of space exploration. What camera and what film did you use to take these pictures, Peter?"

"An *Instamatic* camera with Kodak film."

"Well, Peter, did you know that McLunic also used Kodak film for his photographs in space? His pictures are in color too. Unfortunately, we only have a black-and-white television set! But I have some color slides from the picture series that he made in space which I am going to show to the class now. Slides are photographs which can be shown with a projector."

All the boys, including Peter, were fascinated by the pictures of the earth. It seemed to glow with a bluish light surrounded by the blackness of space. The continents appeared yellow-brown, partly covered by bright, white clouds. All the colors were unbelievably impressive. Mr. Kraus slowly inserted one slide after the other into the projector.

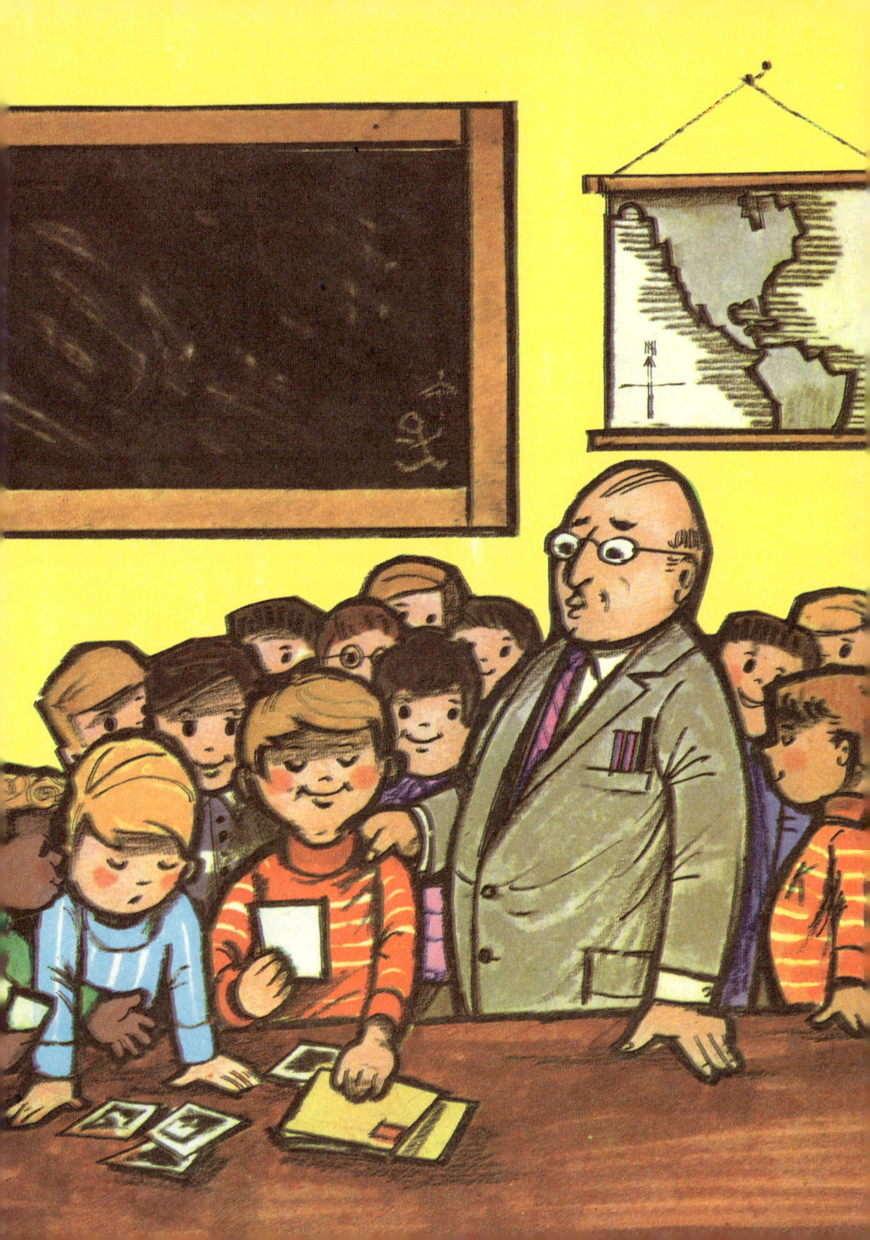

Just then, the bell rang. School was out—at least for the day. Tom and Tim, who sat in the first row so the teacher could keep an eye on them, had already run outside. However, Mr. Kraus kept the rest of the class for a few moments to tell them: "Next Monday, we will be going on our class trip. We won't be able to make a trip into space, but I hope you'll all be happy with a visit to Mountainview Castle."

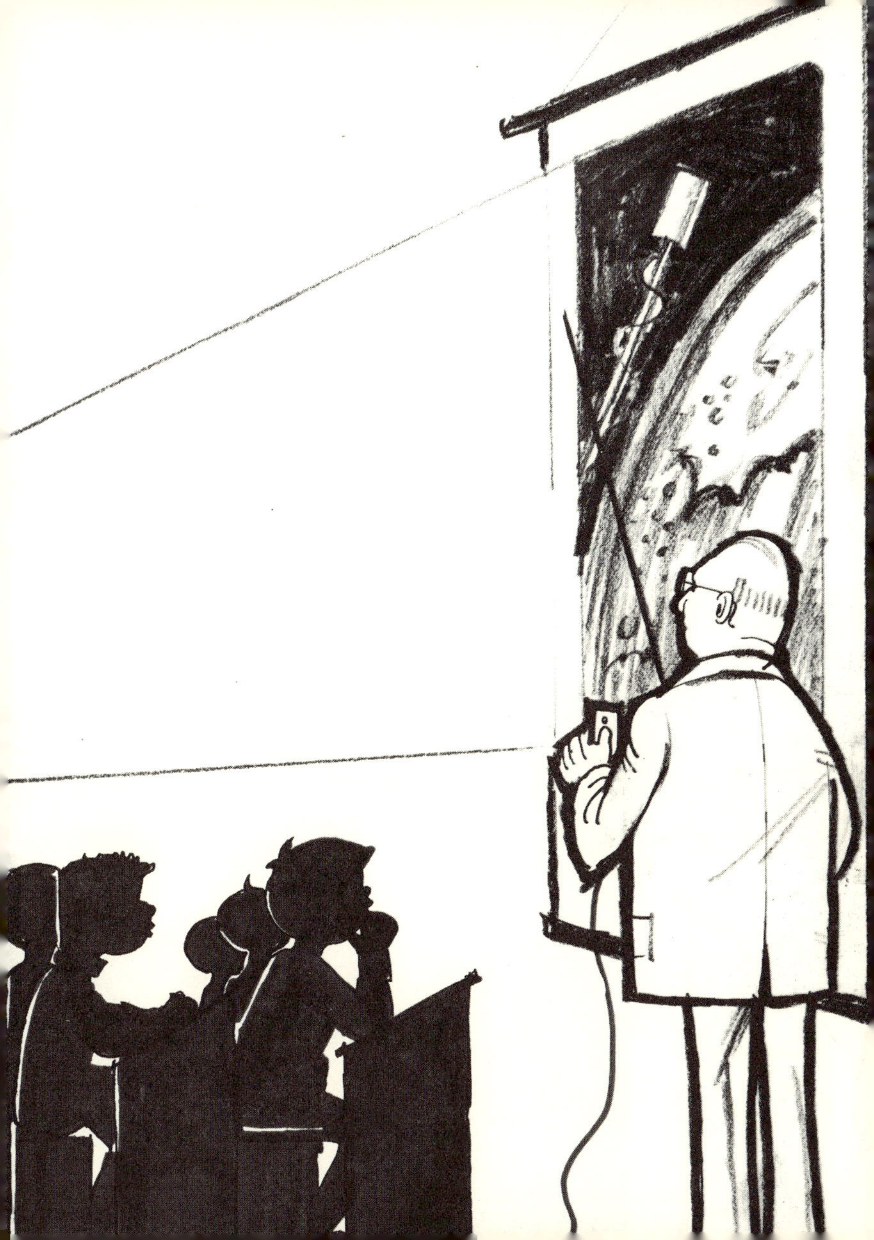

Class trip to Mountainview Castle

At the end of the line at Lindenville, the class got off the bus. Because they would have to walk most of the way without taking the bus or the train, Mr. Kraus agreed to let Peter's dog Skippy come along. Peter also brought along two film cartridges and his magicubes. The class hadn't been walking for more than 15 minutes when Tom and Tim joined Peter. They wanted their picture taken! While Peter was getting ready,

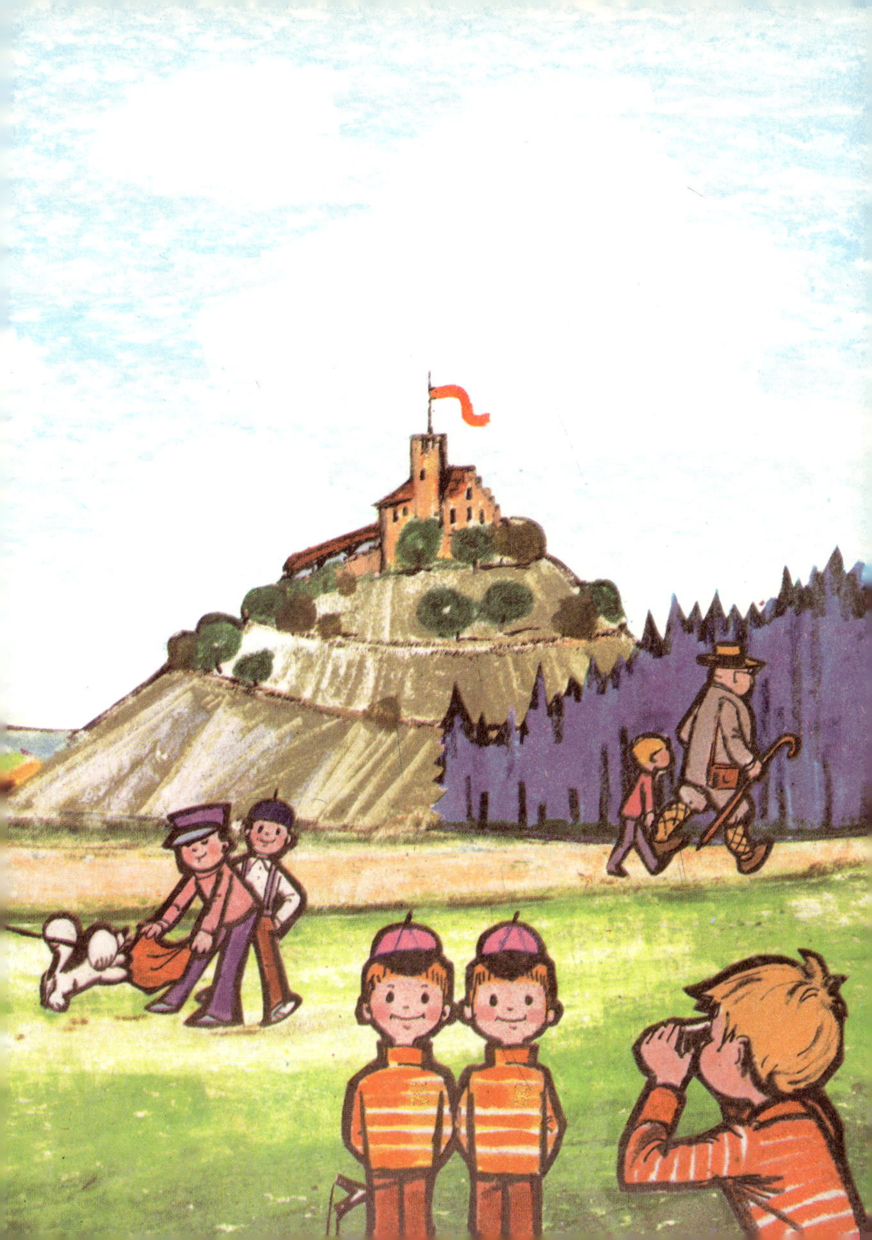

they posed stiffly and made serious faces. Fortunately, Peter had already learned that posed pictures are never as interesting as snapshots taken when the subject is not expecting it. So he played a trick on them: he aimed the camera at the twins, and called out, "Ready—now!" But he didn't really press the button; he merely advanced the film with the lever. That made a convincing little click to fool them. The twins really believed Peter had taken their picture. They quickly relaxed their serious faces and returned to the usual sassy expressions for which they were well-known. That was the moment when Peter really took the picture.

The first rest stop the class took was in the woods. It was not very light under the dense foliage of the trees, so Peter took the precaution of preparing his *Instamatic* camera for flash shots. That was a wise move.

Only a few seconds later he was able to capture his teacher on film. Peter had placed a closeup attachment on his camera to make tiny things look big on the pictures. When Peter pressed the button, Mr. Kraus was lying on his stomach trying to photograph a butterfly.

Up at Mountainview Castle, an unexpected problem occurred. Skippy was usually a very friendly dog but he simply didn't seem to like

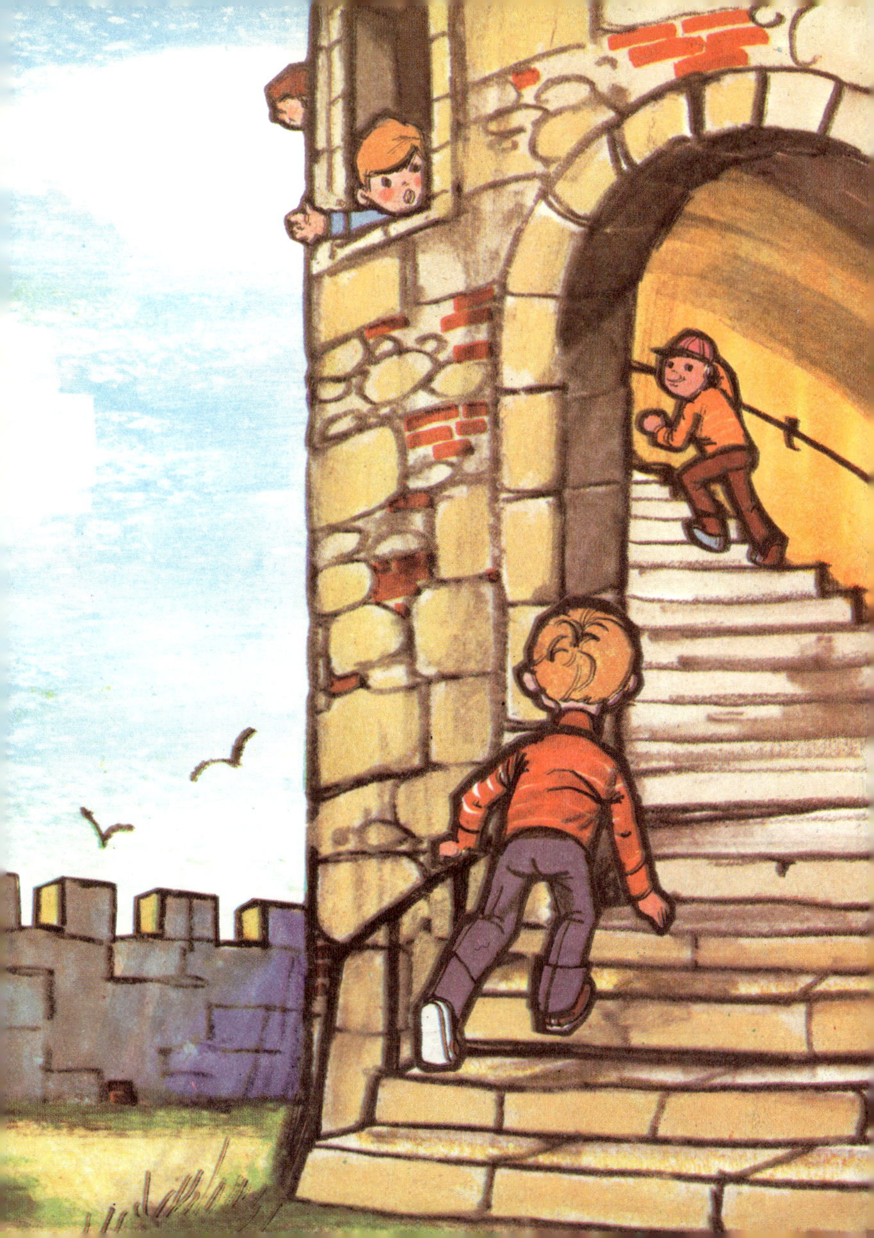

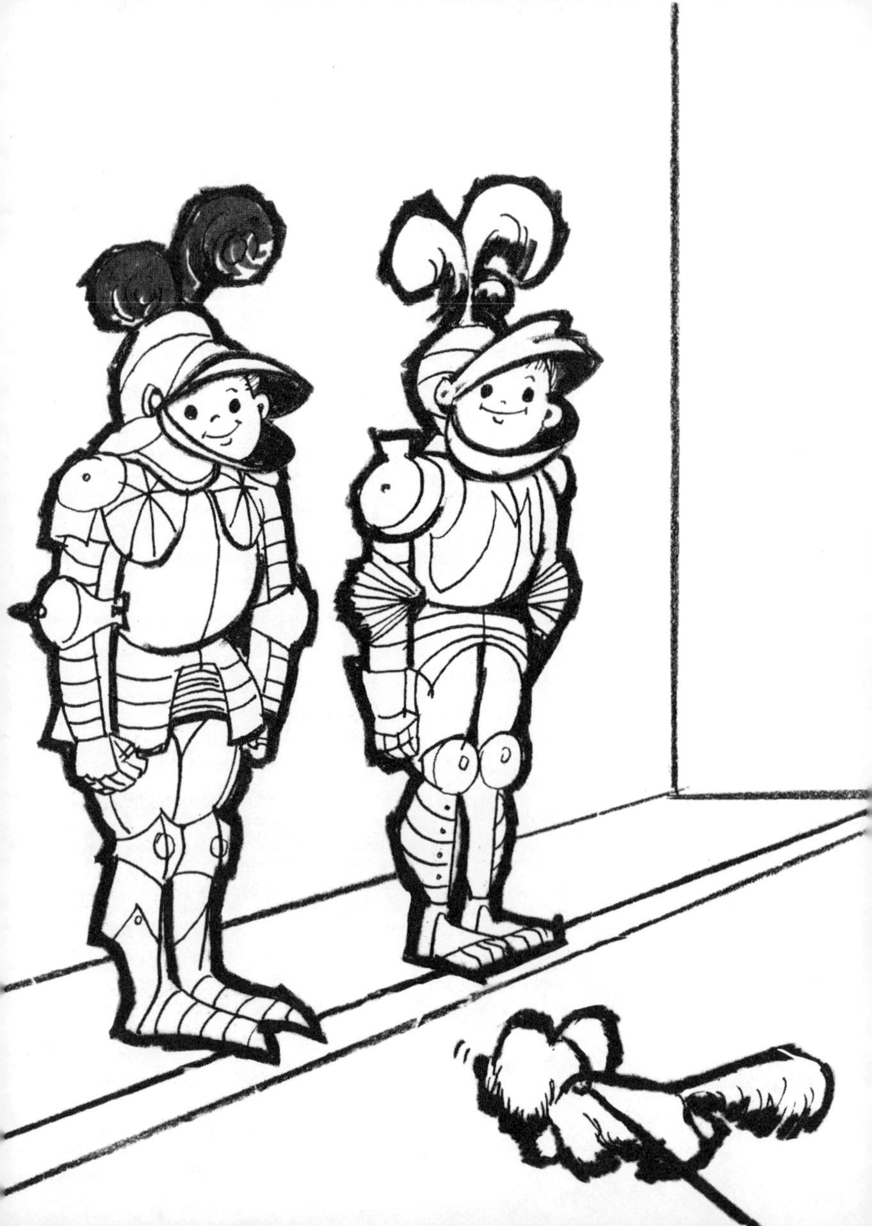

Mr. Leadon, the guide with whom Mr. Kraus was discussing the tour. Peter had to tie the jumping and barking puppy to a tree before starting the visit to the castle.

The wood-paneled walls inside the castle were covered with medieval lances, shields, hunting trophies, and riding gear. In every nook and corner, there were armored suits once used by knights.

What an assortment of rooms, chambers, and banquet halls there were in the castle! Without Mr. Leadon to guide them, the boys would have been hopelessly lost. They were relieved when they got back to the entrance, and Mr. Kraus asked: "Are we all here? Where are Tom and Tim, the twins?" They didn't seem to be around. Only Tom's cap—or was it Tim's—was lying near the door.

"I know they came with us," said Peter, "because I saw them!"

"And they would not be able to leave during the tour," added Mr. Leadon, "because everything is locked." Where could they be?

The children, the tour guide, and the teacher spread out to look for them. They searched the entire castle from top to bottom. Not a trace of Tom! Not a trace of Tim! What should they do? Mr. Kraus wiped his worried brow with a handkerchief. After all, the pupils were his responsibility.

But Peter had the best idea: "Why not let Skippy look for them?"

Peter let Skippy sniff the cap that was near the door, and then followed behind him holding a long leash. At the castle staircase, Skippy unexpectedly began to jump against a suit of armor and started barking so that the sound echoed through all the passages of the castle. What could be the matter with him? Suddenly there was a creaky noise like a rusty old hinge. Squeak! The visor of the helmet slowly rose. A pair of sparkling eyes peeked out. Peter was startled.

"Don't be afraid, boys," said their teacher, "I think I know what's going on here! I think it's our Tom!" At that moment the visor of the other suit rose up and Tim peeked out. Mr. Leadon's mouth dropped open, and he asked angrily, "What's the meaning of this? Our priceless armor outfits! I hold the school responsible for any damages!"

All of a sudden there was a flash of light and then another.

It was Peter who didn't want to miss getting a picture of this scene: Tom and Tim as noble knights! With the camera flash, he inadvertently saved the situation. The angry guide quickly became more friendly. He placed himself between the two "knights" and asked Peter to take a picture of him too.

"But be sure to send me a print!"

Mr. Kraus eagerly promised to see that one was sent to him. He was happy that everything had turned out well after all.

As they stood outside the castle, Mr. Kraus told his pupils, "You see, photography is good for many things! Who knows what would have happened if Peter hadn't reached for his camera!"

"We would really be in a fix," said Tom. Tim poked him in the side, "Be quiet, otherwise we might still get punished."

At that moment, another incident took place. Skippy thought that Tom's poke at Tim was an invitation to play. He jumped on Tom's back, knocking him over. There lay the mischievous boy flat on his tummy in the grass, and standing on top of him like a hero was that little ball of wool, Skippy. Peter grabbed his camera again. He just had to capture this hilarious scene.

Peter came home very tired. He had used up ten flashes and had taken 24 snapshots. Tomorrow he would take the two films to be processed. Just before falling asleep, he thought about the many, many pictures he had taken that day. He was especially curious to see how the snapshot of Skippy would turn out.

He hoped to get a photo album for his birthday so that he could insert all of his snapshots. And when he had filled the whole album, he would have a real picture book—a book that he had made himself.

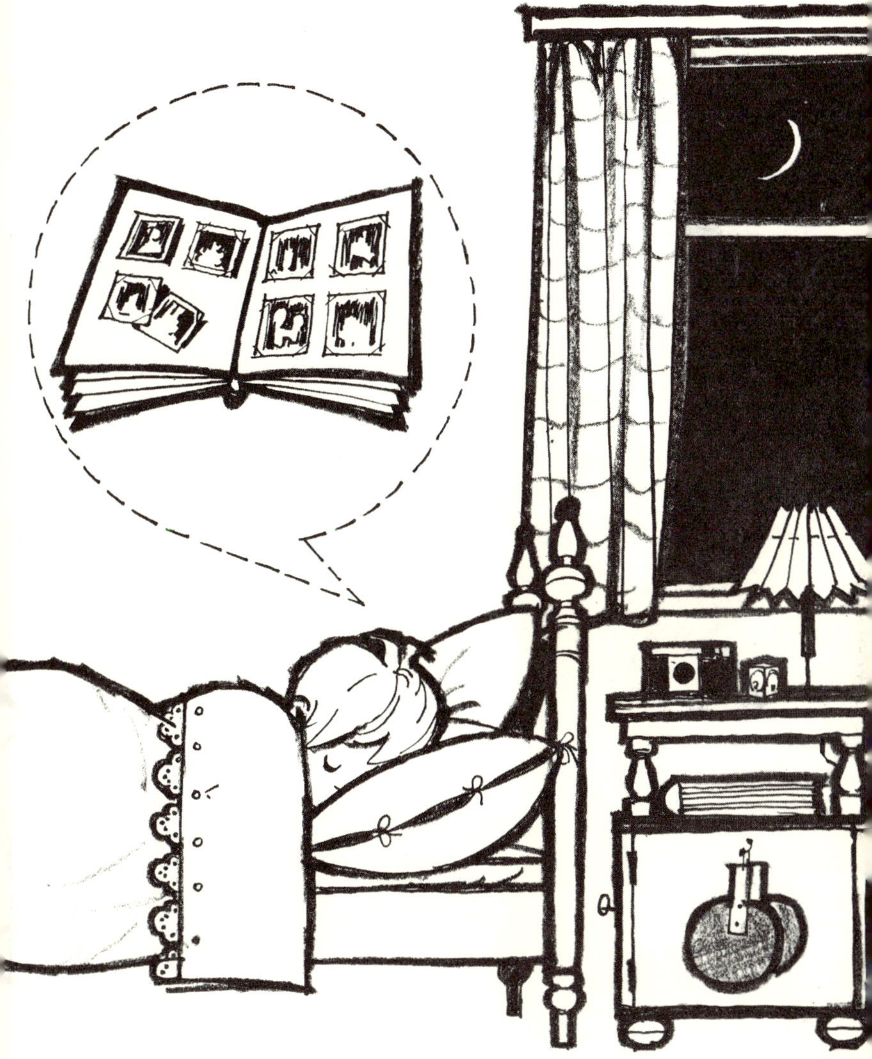

What Peter does to take good pictures

He knows he needs enough light for picture-taking. If Peter wants to take pictures at twilight, in the dark, or indoors, he uses a magicube.

Peter gets as close as possible to his subject to get a really good picture. With his *Kodak Instamatic* camera, he can come as close as 4 feet.

He also watches his distance from his subject when he uses a flash: with magicubes the distance is 4 to 9 feet.

During the exposure, he holds the camera steady. If he is excited, he looks for a wall, a table, or anything else to help him steady his hand.

Fingerprints or dust on the lens can ruin the best pictures. So Peter occasionally cleans his lens by blowing away any dust or dirt and using a soft, lens tissue.

He also pays attention to the background and tries to avoid telephone poles, fence posts, overhead wires. The background should not be distracting.

Peter also discovered that candid snapshots are far more interesting than posed pictures. That's why he tries to photograph his unsuspecting "victims" before they realize it. But if Peter does take a posed picture, he asks his subjects to read, to play, or to do something. That way he gets a better picture.

Terms used by camera fans

"ASA" speed
The sensitivity of film is indicated by the "ASA" speed. The higher the "ASA" number, the greater the sensitivity of the film. ASA 64 is the value for film of normal sensitivity.

Battery
This is a unit which stores electric current. It is used in the camera or in the flash holder. Some flashcubes, like light bulbs, need electricity to light up. And that comes from the batteries.

Cameras
Photographic devices in which films can be exposed are called "cameras."

Close-up attachment
For pictures of butterflies and other small things, special attachments are needed. Without such attachments, you can only come as close as four feet with an *Instamatic* camera.

Depth of field
This is the range of distances in which everything will appear sharp. The depth of field in *Instamatic* cameras is from four feet to infinity.

Double exposure prevention
If you cannot press the release button twice in a row without advancing the film, then the camera has double exposure prevention; this prevents the same piece of film from being exposed twice.

Ektachrome film
The name of a popular Kodak color slide film.

Enlargement

Our subjects usually appear much smaller on the film than they do on the paper prints that we get back from the camera shop. In other words, every picture has been slightly enlarged. If you like a certain picture particularly well, a postcard-size (or even larger) enlargement can be made.

Exposure time

At the moment a photograph is taken, the camera's shutter opens for a very short time—for instance, about 1/90th of a second. This short time is the exposure time.

Film

The camera has to be loaded with film. Several pictures can always be made on one roll of film. After processing the film, the pictures appear as negatives or as positive transparencies called "slides."

Film advance

A mechanism to advance the film inside the camera is called the "film advance." After each exposure, a section of new unexposed film is moved into position behind the lens. The film advance is operated by a lever. So that you do not forget to advance the film, every *Instamatic* camera has double exposure prevention.

Film cartridge
This is a plastic container loaded with film which can be easily placed in *Instamatic* cameras. Most Kodak film cartridges contain 12 exposures. Color film cartridges are also available with 20 exposures.

Fixed focus
This term means that the lens on the camera has been focused at a particular distance. That's why you never have to set the distance yourself on a fixed focus camera. Everything is sharp from four feet to infinity.

Flashbulbs
These are small bulbs which give off a very short but bright flash of light. With their help, we can take pictures indoors or outdoors at night. Flashbulbs are used in flash holders with reflectors.

Flashcubes
These cubes contain four small bulbs and four reflectors. Therefore, four flash pictures can be taken quickly one after the other. Flashcubes require batteries to flash. See "Magicubes," also.

Instamatic cameras
The name of a line of easy-to-use cameras made by Eastman Kodak Company.

Kodachrome film
The name of a Kodak color slide film.

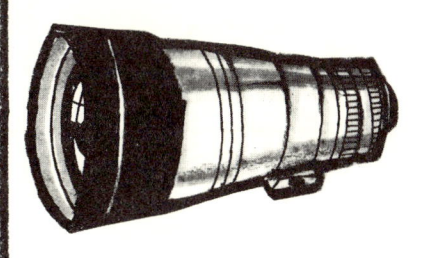

Kodacolor II film
The name of a Kodak color negative film from which color prints can be made.

Lens
A round piece of specially designed glass or plastic through which light enters the camera to form an image on the film. The lenses on most cameras consist of several pieces of lens material put together.

Magicubes
Magicubes are similar to flashcubes, except that magicubes do not need batteries to flash. The two types of cubes are not interchangeable because cameras are designed to use only one kind of cube. See your camera instruction manual.

Negative
This is the name for some types of film after they have been developed and fixed. There are negatives from black-and-white film and also from color film. From color film, prints can be made in black-and-white and in color. The colors on a negative are reversed; for instance, a white horse looks like a black horse on a negative. But on the paper prints which are made from these negatives, the colors are correct again. Colored negative films come back as negatives and colored slide films come back as cardboard mounted slides.

Pictures against the sun

When the sun shines at the back of your subject, it also shines on the front of your camera. Such scenes can be very pretty. But we have to be very careful that the sun does not shine right on the lens during the exposure.

Processing

After all the pictures on the film have been exposed, it has to be processed. First it is placed in a developing solution. This makes the picture visible. Then the film is placed in another solution called the "fixer," which preserves the image.

Reflector

A curved mirror which directs reflected light back to the subject is called a "reflector." Flashbulb holders include a reflector. In magicubes and flashcubes, the reflectors are built-in.

Sensitivity

In the old days, film and plates required long exposure times; they had low sensitivity. Today's films, however, only need a little light. They have greater sensitivity.

Shutter

The shutter keeps light from passing through the camera lens. It only opens during the exposure to let light enter through the lens for a brief moment.

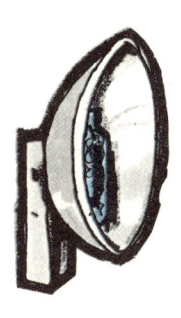

Shutter release
This is the button on the top of the camera which we press when we want to snap the picture. If a flash attachment is used, it is triggered at the same time.

Slide
When this type of film is processed, it shows the finished picture only when held up to the light. It is a positive transparency, not a negative. For viewing slides, the projector uses a light to throw a picture on a screen or a wall.

Slide projector
This is a device with which transparencies—also called "slides"—are projected on a screen.

Telephoto lens
On some cameras, the lenses can be interchanged. A telephoto lens works like a telescope to make distant subjects look closer.

Tripod
A support for the camera, usually with three legs, is known as a "tripod."

Verichrome pan film
The name of a Kodak black-and-white film.

Wide-angle lens
This interchangeable lens is used when we cannot move far enough away from the subject to get it all into the picture.

Astronaut McRunic

Reporter Kelly

Mr. Boller

Officer Pry